Photo Courtesy of: *Austin American Statesman*

What Once Seemed Strange
A Memoir of Egyptian Exile from Cairo to Austin

by Michele Kay with Mary Ann Roser

Edited by Catherine Rainwater

BanyanTreePress.com

What Once Seemed Strange
A Memoir of Egyptian Exile
from Cairo to Austin

by Michele Kay with Mary Ann Roser

Edited by Catherine Rainwater

ISBN: 9781936449583

Library of Congress Control Number: 2013950478

Banyan Tree Press

www.banyantreepress.com

Englewood, Colorado

Austin, Texas

Cover/Interior by: DPMediaPro.com

Printed in U.S.A

Endorsements and Tributes

Repeatedly displaced from the age of 12, Michele shines through. Nicely paced. The spread of topics and the flow are well managed: just the right mix of adventure, movement, and description balanced with introspection of what she learned, forced to move among four continents and living in eight of the world's major cities. Truly, a gripping story. A tribute to perseverance.

Ken Ashworth,
Austin, Texas
Retired Commissioner of the Higher Education Coordinating Board, Professor at University of Texas and Texas A&M. Author of *On the Horns of a Dilemma, Caught Between the Dog and the Fireplug,* and other books

I, like everyone who knew Michele, always suspected that her story was as interesting as any of the thousands she told during her remarkable career in journalism. I was wrong. Her story is more interesting than any she told. It's a fascinating look at how events that changed the world impacted one person, creating a unique woman who we lost too soon but who left an indelible imprint on so many. Thanks, Michele, for sharing this with us.

Ken Herman,
Austin, Texas
Pulitzer Prize winning Journalist
Columnist, *Austin-American-Statesman*

By the time Michelle Kay was 23, she'd been escorted by armed guards out of Egypt, lived in Paris, Hong Kong, Saigon, New York, London, San Francisco and Cairo, learned to drink Scotch and smoke tobacco with Aussie journalists covering Asia, married a combat cameraman and birthed a baby girl after a mad dash by plane out of Vietnam. And that was just the beginning of a life that was both too much and too short. Michelle died when she was only 67, but she left behind this story, one of an unforgettable person and an extraordinary time.

Bill Bishop
Austin, Texas
Author of *The Big Sort,*
New York Times Best Seller

As a journalist, Michele Kay often wrote and spoke in deceptively simple and straightforward ways, "deceptive" because her word choices revealed such profound and precise understanding, honesty, and experience. Now, thanks to Michele's final efforts and those of dedicated friends and her beloved husband, we have a life narrative told with the same unstinting honesty and transparency. Here we see the effects of displacement on her family, banished from their Egyptian home in 1956 and navigating their changed circumstances in both Europe and Asia. Michele writes about identity, loss, adjustment, and renewal--her own as well as her family's--with a rare awareness and grace. Hers is a remarkable story, told with an authenticity that deepens our knowledge of the human desire to explore and cultivate places of belonging in the world.

Paula Marks, PhD.
Austin, Texas
Professor of American Studies
St. Edward's University

Not everyone who is worth reading about was famous and not everyone who is or was famous is worth reading about. It is unusual to find someone as tough and smart and just flat-out interesting as Michele Kay. She was like a book of short stories come alive. No matter how much we talked, there was always another unexpected and wonderful tale or experience to hear. We are lucky she wrote some of it down for us.

Ross Ramsey,
Austin, Texas
Executive Editor, *The Texas Tribune*

Journalist Michele Kay's signature characteristic, apart from her boundless energy, was her talent for friendship. If you belonged to the Friends of Michele tribe, you were assured of her complete attention, empathy, and willingness to drop everything to rush to your aid if needed. A self-styled "headhunter," Michele would canvass her wide-ranging networks to secure a job for many a friend – in my case two editorial jobs with magazines in Hong Kong. If you are not yet a member of this fortunate tribe, you will feel as though you've been initiated and welcomed after reading this unforgettable memoir of a remarkable woman who packed multiple lives into one.

Carrie Rosenthal
Atlanta, Georgia
Former Editor, *Reader's Digest*

Michele Kay was a mentor to me and a role model and a friend. Never before has so much life been packed into such a small space. This book looks beyond her gale-force personality and explains how she was profoundly shaped by a convulsing Middle East. But her displacement, which she struggled with for most of her life, was our gain, in that it took her to Europe, to Asia and, finally, to the Hill Country of Texas, which is where she and I met. Reading this book made me miss Michele all over again. But it also reminded me anew of how extraordinary she was, as a survivor, a beloved mother, wife, friend and colleague -- and as a writer.

Kyle Pope
New York City, New York
Former reporter at the *Austin American-Statesman*, Editing positions at *Newsweek, Vanity Fair* and *The Wall Street Journal*

Having known Michele as both a personal friend and a target for her political reporting, I find this a remarkable life story. Given her life experiences I now understand why she seemed to know the answer to her question before I answered then proceeded to, while presenting my answer, explain the issue in a way few could. We all miss you Michele, both as a friend and great journalist.

Bruce Todd
Austin, Texas
Travis County Commissioner
Former Austin Mayor

Table of Contents

Dedication

For Robert, with love and gratitude . . .

One day, the immigrant suddenly realizes that she has changed. Something happens that would previously have made her stop and shake her head.

What once seemed strange is now commonplace . . .

Michele Kay

Preface—A Note on the Text

*M*any hands have touched this final manuscript, written mostly by Michele herself, but also shaped, edited, and proofread by Catherine Rainwater, Mary Ann Roser, Joanna Hitchcock, and Robert Schultz.

For all of us, it was a labor of love. Michele, we hope you like it. *Dans un monde si plein d'amis, tu n'étais jamais—une étrangère.*

Catherine Rainwater
Professor of English, St. Edward's
University, Austin, Texas

Foreword

Almost everyone who heard Michele Kay talk about her life had the same reaction: You must write a book. Michele would listen politely and then change the subject. As a journalist throughout almost her entire career, she was used to telling other peoples' stories—not her own. It wasn't until Michele left her newspaper job at the *Austin American-Statesman* in 2003, earned a bachelor's degree at St. Edward's University and, in short order, a master's degree, that she finally wrote about her remarkable life.

Using her descriptive powers as a journalist and her formidable intellect, she wrote a series of nonfiction literary essays chronicling her family's exile from Egypt in 1956 and the effects of displacement on their lives. She wove their personal stories onto a historical fabric, beginning with the Suez Canal Crisis, which transformed Middle Eastern and European politics. The essays formed her master's thesis project, directed by Catherine Rainwater, a professor of English at St. Edward's who eventually became a close friend, and who would also edit the manuscript that Michele finally produced.

However, Michele left out a lot, too. She did not write in great detail about herself. And while she wrote an extraordinarily personal and riveting essay about her brother, Jean-Pierre Trigaci, she did not include similar essays about her parents.

Although I had met Michele in late 1995, I knew only fragments of her life story. She was endlessly curious about others, and a great one for turning the tables and asking people questions about themselves whenever the spotlight was cast in her direction.

When I had the privilege of reading her thesis—something few people outside her St. Edward's community had ever seen—I hungered to know more. I urged Michele when she retired from St. Edward's in 2008 to carve out some time for expanding the thesis into a memoir. She said she wanted to do that, too, but in typical Michele fashion she was very busy in her retirement, traveling, entertaining and looking for projects to get involved in. The book could wait.

But then she was diagnosed with a lethal brain tumor. Most tragically, it was in the temporal lobe, the seat of speech and memory. Surgery and chemotherapy ensued; then, shocking recurrences and more surgery.

Michele had no illusions about surviving the cancer. She knew her time was short. We talked about the memoir. Was there a way I could help her get started? She suddenly was interested. She wanted a legacy for her husband, children and grandchildren. She would work on it, she promised. She would let me know if I could help. But she was exhausted and some days she was asleep more than she was awake. It soon became clear that she was having problems reading and writing; she simply was not up to the task.

Michele could still talk, though. And while her short-term memory was starting to fade, her remembrances of events long past remained sharp. Would she be open to my interviewing her and allowing me to write up what she had said? I would read back to her what I had a written to make sure she agreed with the wording. After I was confident I had enough for an essay, we would edit it together. She immediately said yes. I cannot say how delighted I was. For one thing, Michele was fiercely independent and stubborn. To accept help, however small, was a big deal; she never wanted to put anyone out. I felt privileged. I not only had a standing date to visit her weekly, but working on the essays would give me a view I had never had into her amazing life.

We agreed to keep the topic focused as much as possible on her family's displacement to carry on the theme she had begun in her master's thesis.

Starting in March 2010, a year after she was diagnosed with brain cancer, we met almost every Saturday in her home office. I looked forward to our meetings all week. I hoped I was asking the right questions. In crafting the essays, I would use her words in my writing whenever possible so the stories would retain her voice. We started with her mother's life. I would sit mesmerized by Michele's storytelling, sometimes forgetting to start the tape recorder. Inevitably, the phone would ring—she answered any ringing phone without fail—and only then would the spell be broken. Often, it was Jean-Pierre, and Michele would converse with him for five or ten minutes in flawless French.

Within a couple of months, I had enough to write her mother's essay and read it back to her. Michele was pleased. I felt I had passed a crucial test. We were going to move on her to her father's story next, but Michele's speech was faltering and I worried that her memory might be next. I suggested we work on her own story and defer her father's essay until later. She agreed, although there were times when she would say in all seriousness: "I don't want this to be all about me."

It took several months to get Michele's story, and although I started writing the essay about her, I thought it best to interview her about her father while she could still speak and remember. We finished those interviews and I went back to writing her essay. I read pieces of it back to her. She was always generous in her praise and made few changes.

We talked about writing about her children and the effects of displacement on their lives. But time was running short, and Michele said that her children could tell their own stories better than she could. Her parents were different. They were both gone, and Michele wanted their histories recorded.

I was halfway finished writing the essay about Michele's life and reading it back to her when she went into the hospital in November 2010 with a severe brain infection. We never had a chance to work on the essays after that. It was up to me to finish writing her story and her father's essay.

By January 2011, I had finished writing Michele's essay and was starting the one on her father, Tony. Michele had lost her ability to speak, and it was not clear how much conversation she was able to follow. It did not matter, though. I would read both pieces to her anyway, as I had promised. But before I could, I had to go to Cincinnati to help care for my mother, who had broken her hip. I took my laptop so I could finish Tony's essay there, and I finally did, the night before I flew back to Austin on February 15. I planned to call Michele the next day and make plans to read it back to her at her bedside when she felt up for a visit. It no longer mattered to me whether she could follow along or not. The only thing that mattered was finishing together what we had started. That morning, on February 16, Michele's husband, Robert Schultz, called before I had a chance to call their home: Michele had just died.

By then, there were three new essays to integrate into Michele's master's thesis and re-form into this memoir. Thankfully, Michele had had the wisdom months earlier, while she was still able to speak, to contact her friend Catherine and ask if she would be willing, once again, to be her editor. Catherine generously agreed. I sent the finished essays to Catherine, and she masterfully wedded the pieces together. She took out the many redundancies I had added in the retelling of some stories and seamlessly stitched the old material to the new. She honored Michele's desire to keep the focus on displacement and deserves the gratitude of Michele's family and friends for her tireless work. And in her quest for accuracy, she sent the manuscript to Robert and to Michele's dear friend Joanna Hitchcock, a wordsmith who was chief of University of Texas Press. They went through the memoir line by line and made corrections and suggestions.

Michele and I had talked about death and the nefarious effects of brain cancer. I saw it as the ultimate form of displacement in her life. We talked about exploring that in an essay, but we never had the chance. In a way, I am glad we did not dwell on that. Cancer has a way of stealing a person's identity, if you let it. I could tell Michele enjoyed having a mission and focus in her final year that was not defined by her illness. She was always eager to work on the essays with me and was determined to finish the task. It was an escape from all the visits and calls that focused on how she was feeling and what was going to happen next. The work demonstrated repeatedly that her life had meaning, that she had accomplished much and touched many lives. Not everyone's life is as rich or interesting as Michele's, but everyone has a story. She showed me how important it is to write one's stories at the end of life. I would recommend that anyone with an ailing loved one consider doing this as a way to honor the person and receive an unexpectedly rich reward. To be part of that endeavor with Michele has been my greatest honor and the most precious gift I've ever received.

In everlasting gratitude,
Mary Ann Roser

Cairo
1956

Our world came apart in October of 1956, but it was not until December 2, my twelfth birthday, that it collapsed entirely. We were awakened early that morning by a loud bang, followed by the spine-chilling, crushing noise of shattering glass. The intrusion was a shock, but not really a surprise. In fact, for some of us, it was almost a relief.

My family and I had been locked up in our sixth-floor apartment in Cairo for nearly two months waiting for something to happen. Sometimes it seemed to me that almost any kind of change would be acceptable. Some days we dreamed that the siege would end peacefully, and that we would be allowed to resume our normal lives. On other days, the pendulum swung sharply in the opposite direction, and we had little hope.

My father's friend and colleague, Charlie Pittuck, had been arrested several days before we were put under house arrest. He was charged with spying. My mother, brother and I had no idea what had prompted this, but my father, suspecting a connection between Charlie's arrest and our confinement, feared that perhaps he, too, would be arrested. My father, who usually tried so hard to stay cheerful, grew serious.

"They may come, just for me," he said more than once.

That prospect was too frightening even to contemplate, let alone discuss. Most of the time, my parents tried to stay calm and rational.

My father tried to keep us upbeat and entertained. After dinner, he often put on gramophone records and taught us to waltz and to tango. I danced with my father, my brother, Jean-Pierre, with my mother. Sometimes my parents danced with each other. They were a very romantic, dashing couple even during those tumultuous days.

But there was a new undercurrent of worry in their lives that they could not conceal. As it eventually turned out, we would be forced to leave Egypt, and we would go to England, a faraway place none of us could even visualize. It would set in a motion a series of moves and a sense of displacement that would define all of our lives, though in vastly different ways.

"Thank God the children have passports," my father would say.

At the time, I did not understand what he meant. By the second month of our confinement, the tension had become unbearable. We sat. We paced. Sometimes my parents talked in quiet tones. Sometimes they argued, their voices rising.

"At least the children now have passports" was the refrain in every conversation.

Cairo, Under House Arrest
1956

A typewriter and an international code-signaling key were the tools of my father's trade. His typewriter was a big, black machine. During our confinement in Cairo, Tony taught my brother and me to use both. He covered the letters on the keys of the typewriter with tiny pieces of paper and made us learn to touch-type. I practiced for hours, and became a fairly proficient typist and international code operator.

"If you can type and know international code, you'll always be able to find a job," my father often told me.

My brother, Jean-Pierre, was interested neither in typing nor in international code. He liked to play cards. While we endured the weeks of house arrest, he played two-deck gin rummy with fourteen cards. This is harder than the conventional ten-card game. Sometimes we played backgammon. My father had a beautiful, ornate set that he let us use. It was hard to play with Jean-Pierre because he was a terrible loser. My mother always asked me to let him win.

"Don't get him upset," she would tell me. "Everyone is upset enough. You don't have to make it worse." When Jean-Pierre lost, he threw the cards on the floor or banged the backgammon set shut. Then he slammed doors with great fanfare and went off to his room in a sulk.

The servants came and went, bringing us food. They set the table with fine linens, china and crystal, but our meals, once shared during large family gatherings, were no longer events or feasts. We did not see or hear from anyone else—not from my mother's family, not from my father's family, not from friends or neighbors. We had a radio, but toward the end of our confinement, the radio was removed, and the phone was cut off. We were isolated and starved for news.

In the days before we came under house arrest, the Egyptian government had tried to wrest control of the Suez Canal from the British and the French. England and France responded by bombing Egyptian military installations. Within days, Israel had joined the fray. The United States initially supported its European allies, but then abruptly changed course and decided to stay out of the battle. That was when our phone went dead, our radio was confiscated and guards began to stand outside our door. Afterward, we no longer knew what was happening in the country, not even on the day we were evicted.

From our balcony that day, everything in Cairo looked normal. The sidewalks were packed with people; tramways, buses and cars jammed the roads. Foul-smelling fumes drifted up the six floors to assail our nostrils, as usual. The imam at the mosque adjacent to our apartment building called people to prayer at regular intervals during the day.

On Fridays, the Muslim Sabbath, the traffic came to a grinding halt as the mosque filled to capacity and men spread their prayer rugs on the street. We could see heads popping up and down, and rear ends suspended in the air. At sunset, we looked out to see the big Egyptian sky colored in pink hues, and in the distance, the outline of the spectacular, perfectly proportioned Great Pyramids of Giza.

At age twelve, I was too young to understand the intricacies of foreign policy. All I knew was that my mother, Paulette, was Jewish and that the Arabs were angry at the Jews. Recently, she had become fearful and distraught. Even before our house arrest, she had started talking to friends and family in anxious whispers.

Still, we heard the familiar refrain about passports. And "Not in front of the children," she would tell visitors.

From House Arrest to Exile
1956

S ince Malta had once been a British colony, my Egyptian-born but Maltese father, Tony, was officially British rather than English. Though the British did not operate Marconi Cable & Wireless, the British owned this company where Tony worked in the telegraph office. Thus, in a roundabout way, he worked for the British government. Back then, the most important communications, including even the most confidential dispatches between government leaders, went through the telegraph office.

When Tony heard that the Egyptians had taken control of the Suez Canal, he became very agitated. I had never seen him that nervous. His two brothers, Carlo and Gino, his sister Alice and her husband, Richard, came often to our apartment; they spent hours engaged in frantic whispering in languages my brother and I did not understand. What we did understand, though, was that Charlie Pittuck, my father's close associate at Marconi Cable & Wireless, had been arrested, and that the adults were relieved about "the children's passports," and that they were hinting about leaving Egypt.

My mother did not want to leave Cairo. She feared that she would never be able to return. She had been born in Egypt and wanted to die there. Her brother-in-law, Teddy—her sister Joujou's husband—had fought for Israel during the War of Independence in 1948, and he had never been allowed back into Cairo. Consequently, he and Joujou lived in Melbourne, Australia. My mother kept telling us that she could not imagine going to live so far away, in such an alien place.

"I don't even know where Australia is," my mother remarked, more to herself than to us.

My brother did not want to leave, either. Jean-Pierre's whole universe was Cairo. Exile would prove to be traumatic for him.

Even though my father, always adaptable, wanted to leave, he wanted to leave in his own time and on his own terms. He told us we would have more opportunities and a better chance of enjoying peace and prosperity in Europe. There was no future for us in Egypt, he insisted. There was no future in the Middle East for Jews, or for anyone who was not Arab.

On the morning that would turn out to be our last one in Cairo, and two months after we had lost all contact with the rest of the family, four armed Egyptian soldiers, rifles slung over their shoulders, stood on the antique red Persian rug in our living room. There was no doubt who was in control. We were going somewhere and it would not be in our own time or on our own terms. The soldiers told us to get dressed and to be quick about it. They inspected the room, the French antiques, the Persian rugs, and the crystal chandeliers with a look of contempt rather than admiration. They shouted at the servants to bring them coffee.

"Don't bother to pack," the oldest of the soldiers said. "You're not taking anything with you."

"Are we leaving the country?" my father asked. I could tell he wanted the answer to be yes.

But the soldier only shrugged. "Get a move on," he said.

My parents, my brother and I rushed to put on clothes, our hands shaking as we tried to close zippers and fasten buttons. We did not speak. We had never talked about what we would wear if we had to leave. We had not dealt with practicalities. Instead, we had kept our predicament suspended in our minds like a sort of mirage, like the illusory pools of water that shimmered always just ahead of us as we drove in the nearby desert.

I saw my mother putting on all the jewelry she owned and covering it up with clothing. She told us to put on layers of clothes, as many as would fit around us. It was December, and if we were going to England, it would be cold. She dressed hurriedly. I had never before seen my mother look dowdy, but she looked so now in an old black skirt and enough sweaters to make her appear top-heavy. Meanwhile, my father stuffed money, papers, and some odd little black books in his jacket pockets.

Jean-Pierre was shaking with rage and fear. His movements were wary but deliberate, as though premeditated. One by one, and quite methodically, he picked up the treasures that lined a shelf of his bedroom and hurled them to the floor—the earthen vases he had bought from the Bedouins on a trip to the desert, the little porcelain figures our aunt Alice had brought back from Greece, and the brightly painted piggy bank in the shape of a kangaroo that our aunt Joujou had sent from Melbourne. Some broke in two, some shattered into dozens of pieces. Glass shards littered the floor.

"Cheri, don't," Paulette implored, trying to put her arms around him. But he pushed her away. He smashed to bits a prized possession, his small rowboat that leaned against the wall in his room. Jean-Pierre had warned me that, when they came, he would break as many of his things as he could. If he could not have them, no one else could have them, either.

I was both terrified and elated. For me, anything was better than the ordeal of confinement we had suffered during the last two months. I could not imagine too many more days of waiting, filling the time with dancing, typing and playing cards. I had traveled out of Egypt only once, when my father had taken Jean-Pierre and me to the mountains outside Beirut, Lebanon, to visit his sister Therese. My mother could not go with us because Jews were not allowed in Lebanon, but I had loved the trip. The mountains were beautiful, the air felt crisp and clean and there were no crowds in the streets. The prospect of a journey to anywhere was enticing, even under threatening circumstances.

My father was pale. He was perspiring heavily, and he was unnaturally quiet. His bottom lip quivered. I thought he might burst into tears, something I had never seen him do. The thought of his crying and not being in charge frightened me. My mother had assumed an uneasy quietude—the kind of stillness that permeates the air before a storm.

We turned our backs on the apartment that had been our home since I was born. We were empty-handed, but there were too many of us to fit into the tiny elevator. One guard rode with my father and brother. Another waited to ride with my mother and me. The other two guards walked down the stairs.

We drove through the streets of Cairo and headed for the airport, where we met with more chaos and confusion. It was winter, but unseasonably warm. Peddlers pushed carts and loudly hawked their food and drinks. Women, holding young children and nursing babies, sat on benches and on the filthy-dirty floor. Armed guards and soldiers swirled everywhere, pushing and shoving the crowds. Men dressed in long white gallabeyas, and sporting red tarbouches (similar to a fez), walked around smoking, waving away the army of flies that filled the air. It was hot, dirty and noisy.

A customs inspector tried to take my mother's engagement and wedding rings. He did not notice her other jewelry. She pulled her hand away.

"Let me see that," the inspector said.

"Leave me alone. Don't touch me," my mother retorted.

My father joined the argument. He shouted at the inspector in Arabic,

"Get your dirty hands off my wife!"

The angry inspector grabbed my father's hand, trying to shake loose the ring my father wore. It was a gold signet with a small red ruby that his long-deceased father had given him. The shouting match became louder and more intense.

"You dirty dogs," my father yelled at the inspector, who finally decided to back off. My father had won the round. The rings themselves mattered, but the victory was more important. My father needed one that day—no matter how small.

A new group of soldiers began ferrying us around. They took us to a lounge where, we were shocked to discover, sat my father's two brothers and their wives, his sister Alice, and her husband, Richard. After a lot of hugging, kissing and crying, my father finally broke down. No, they had not been under house arrest. Yes, they had tried to see us but they were not allowed. Yes, the Suez Canal had fallen into Egyptian hands. Yes, Charlie was still in prison. And now, the Egyptians had rounded up everyone with the surname of Trigaci.

"Thank God the children have passports," my father said.

"You are right. *Hamdel Allah*," Richard said, echoing in Arabic my father's words.

"You don't understanding anything," a frustrated Alice retorted. "It is all *because* of the passports."

My Father, Tony

A ntonius "Tony" Trigaci was the happiest, most optimistic person I have ever known. He always assumed everything would work out fine, and if life was not going well, he would figure out a way to fix it. Despite his humble origins and some catastrophic setbacks, he responded to every challenge by figuring out how to meet it successfully. If ever he was discouraged or confused, he never showed it. My father seemed indomitable.

Tony's own father died before I was born. I do not know much about my grandfather Josephi. He was born either in Smyrna or in Malta. I am sure he worked in farming, but he also had some background in engineering, which no doubt prompted his move to Egypt to work in that field. Throughout the Mediterranean, the people are transient. If they see an opportunity, they pick up and go. Travel between Malta, southern Italy, and the Middle East is commonplace, and everyone speaks a variety of languages. My father spoke five— French, Greek, English, Italian and Arabic.

Tony's mother, Stellae Lerioti Trigaci, was Greek. His father had originally married a woman from Malta and brought her to Egypt, but the marriage did not work out, partly because she was unable to have children. On a vacation, Tony's father met the woman who became my grandmother. I am not sure my grandfather ever got a divorce from his Maltese wife—the Catholic Church forbade divorce—but he and my grandmother married and eventually had seven children. There were, in fact, more than these seven, but not all of them survived. My name for Tony's mother was *Yayaka*, a Greek word for "grandmother." I remember her as a smiley lady.

Tony was born in Egypt on March 4, 1911. He always said he was happy, even though his family was poor. Tony loved soccer and played a lot of it. Only about five-feet-six-inches tall, he was nevertheless strong and athletic. He was always telling jokes. He was a tease, and people liked him. None of his family had grand ambitions, although my father said his sisters were all very devout Catholics with lofty spiritual aspirations. Alice wanted to be a nun, but my grandfather frowned on that. He told his girls they should marry well-to-do husbands and have children. One daughter married and had a girl; two others had one boy each. As far as I know, my father was the only one of the siblings to have more than one child.

Unlike his sisters, Tony was not interested in religion. After he completed high school, his thoughts turned toward making his way in the world. My father was clearheaded and practical. If someone said to him, "This is important for us to do," he would pace the floor all night, if need be, to figure out how to make it happen. He was not an intellectual, a reader, or a deep thinker. However, he was definitely street-smart.

He also tended to be progressive in his thinking, unlike his brothers and sisters, who were "old world." Tony kept up with current affairs and was eager to learn about the changing world around him.

I remember in 1957, our first year in London, when the Russians launched Sputnik. The center of London was full of people, and my father was so excited that he took me there to be a part of the history-making moment. Tony was interested in events that happened years ago, but he was not the least bit interested in living in the past.

My father was debonair and romantic with my mother. I think he adored my mother, Paulette, because she was so difficult, and I think she appreciated him because he was so easygoing. Perhaps that is why their marriage worked so well. Sometimes they screamed at each other, but that is very Middle Eastern. When you are Middle Eastern and you get upset, you scream, even when it is about nothing. An argument might be about a triviality—"My watch says two o'clock, but yours says ten after. Which is right?" And the next thing you know, you are screaming over it. But just as quickly, the fire is out and the argument is finished.

My father's fiery passion for my mother, however, was never extinguished. Tony would return from his job at Marconi Cable & Wireless every twelve hours, sometimes at night, sometimes during the day. Either way, whenever his shift ended, he would come home and my parents would go into their bedroom. They would lock themselves in. We kids knew not to disturb them. The rest of the time, my father was happy to have us around.

I loved my father very dearly. All my life, I felt drawn to him. We were simpatico. My father taught me to type. He taught me to dance. He taught me so many other things. Years would pass before I understood all that he sacrificed for me.

My Mother, Paulette

*P*aulette Trigaci was not pretty, but she was elegant and knew exactly how to make the most of her attributes. Standing at five feet, three inches tall, she was always beautifully dressed and impeccably manicured. She was intelligent and well-read, but she had no interest in higher learning. She had an eighth- or ninth-grade education, and that was enough for her. She liked to read novels and history but, like many women in her day, what she cared about most was how she looked. She never left the house without her nice clothes on, her hair styled and a fresh coat of lipstick. Her short, curly hair was dark brown until she let it go gray, but this was no sign she had surrendered her vanity. Part of the graying was a result of typhoid, which she had contracted in her late thirties. While she was ill, her head was shaved, and when her hair grew back gray, she no longer dyed it. She was not vain about her hair color, but to her dying day, at age ninety-three, she never once washed her own hair. Paulette believed that hair washing must be done at the beauty salon.

My mother was used to being taken care of by others. Her parents pampered her. My father doted on her. As a result, the life ahead of her following the events in Cairo in 1956 would be especially tough. She would never fully recover from being exiled from Egypt.

Paulette—Pauletta Harari—was born in Cairo on April 29, 1913, the first of three girls in a Jewish family. The Jews never had it particularly easy in Egypt. Because they held most of the wealth, the Jews were greatly resented. The vast majority of Egyptians, namely the Arab Muslims and the Coptic Christians, were not wealthy. However, all three groups co-existed, mostly peacefully after the middle of the seventeenth century, until tensions between Jews and Christians heated up in Egypt during the early decades of the twentieth century. Anti-Semitism spread like a flu pandemic across Europe and other parts of the world.

Although my mother's family was not rich, they were comfortable. Paulette's father, Nathan Harari, was a successful merchant in Cairo who imported and exported whatever was selling at the time. Short, dark-haired and soft-spoken, he enjoyed socializing with his cronies. He would go to the café in the morning and play backgammon before starting his day, and then spend the rest of it wheeling and dealing.

The family lived with servants in a swanky three-bedroom apartment in the heart of Cairo. As a girl, Paulette didn't have to do anything around the house. And she never worked outside of it. She believed a woman should marry someone who could support her in the comfortable life she enjoyed. Her job was to be an attractive wife.

Paulette met my father, Tony, in the tiny elevator of the building where she and her family lived. He was there for a business appointment. One look at the woman who would become my mother ignited a vigorous pursuit and a lifelong devotion. They were in their early twenties.

Tony Trigaci was always laughing, gregarious and winsome. He was dark-haired, with a receding hairline, high cheekbones and a quick smile. His sunny personality contrasted with my mother's darker, more pessimistic disposition. But right away, they clicked.

Both sets of parents opposed the match, mainly owing to religious differences. Tony was Roman Catholic and had no interest in converting to Judaism. Another problem was that Tony worked for the British government's telegraph company, taking down messages. Paulette's family thought he was never going to be a great provider.

The couple's attraction to one another was strong, however. They were happy together, and determined to be married. Despite their families' opposition, they wed in the Catholic Church on August 27, 1936. The service took place at a side altar. No one attended, not the Jews on my mother's side or the Catholics on my father's side. Undaunted, they honeymooned on the island of Rhodes, in the southern Mediterranean. A black-and-white photograph shows my deeply tanned father carrying my slender mother in his arms on the beach, her curly hair cropped short, her arms encircling his neck.

Tony and Paulette

After my parents' honeymoon in 1936, they moved in with my mother's family, who had finally accepted her groom. My family has always been this way. Once you are married, you are family, no matter what has gone on before. My parents moved into the main bedroom of the apartment where my mother had grown up. And my grandparents moved into two other rooms. Later, when my brother and I came along, we would share a room. And when my grandfather died, my brother got his room, and I moved in with my grandmother Camille.

Before Jean-Pierre and I were born, however, political forces were already at play that would one day upset the balance of world powers and change our lives forever. During the years immediately following my parents' marriage, the Germans occupied Libya, just across the border from Egypt, and they were threatening to attack the Jews. Jews were afraid to have children because they feared they were going to be exterminated by the Germans. Nevertheless, my mother learned she was pregnant soon after the wedding. She gave birth to Jean-Pierre, but as the tensions grew, she was afraid to have more children. Terrified by Hitler and the Germans, she had two abortions over the next four years as she pondered, "Why is God doing this to us?" Paulette never spoke of the abortions, but my grandmother told me why there are five years and no other children between Jean-Pierre and me.

As Nazi aggression increased, Paulette and Tony constantly hid in basements. Finally, after the battle of El Alamein, when the British halted Germany's ambitions in North Africa, they no longer were afraid. I was born in 1944. My mother would often say, "Life then was very difficult." But in hard times, she would always reassure me, "Miche, life will go back to being good."

For a while, my family's lives in Egypt did go back to being good. Life was relatively easy from 1945 to 1956. Paulette was happy. She laughed a lot. She went to the country club.

Jean-Pierre was by far the most important person in her life. He was The Messiah, or at least that is what I eventually called him, to the consternation of my mother. Oddly, Jean-Pierre does not remember my mother as being all that cheerful in Egypt.

No doubt, at times she must have been unhappy, but she was a traditional wife and loved the role. She and Tony went out frequently, and they entertained at home. The Egyptians kept a distance, so we socialized mainly with family. At home, on Friday nights and Saturdays, we were Jewish. On Sundays, we were Catholic. I thought this was a normal arrangement.

Religion infused our lives starting Friday mornings when the Muslims gathered to pray. Half the town emptied out, but the mosque was full. The Muslims chanted, *Allahu Akbar,* or "God is great," over and over. On Friday night, the Jews all gathered around a big meal of chicken and rice, and said prayers at home. On Saturday evenings, when the Jewish prayers began, my Catholic father discreetly disappeared from the beautifully set dinner table. He wouldn't come back until the prayers were over.

Even so, there was no tension between my parents over religion, partly because they were not particularly zealous in their faith. My mother, in fact, had little knowledge about the rituals she practiced. She was born a Sephardic Jew. For Paulette, Judaism was a cultural identity, a tradition ingrained in her, rather than a spiritual path. My father's devotion to Roman Catholicism was comparably tepid. Like Paulette's, it was a faith he had unquestioningly accepted because it was passed down to him through family.

Our placid existence came to an end, however, when all hell broke loose in Egypt, and consequently in my family. Before 1956, of course, there had been signs that not all was right in the country. After King Farouk had been thrown out of power in 1952, the new president, Gamal Nasser, had begun making changes designed to give Arabs a greater say in politics and government. I remember unrest, and I recall angry mobs burning buildings, including part of ours in Cairo. We were trapped in our sixth-floor apartment as the fire reached toward us, higher and higher. It stopped on the third floor but, by then, my parents were in a panic. Fires had been breaking out all over Cairo. All were set deliberately by people loyal to Prime Minister Naguib. The big hotels, office buildings, foreign corporations and residences of well-to-do people were targets. The night the fire came to us was the first time it struck me that things I had no control over could have a profound effect on my life.

Our apartment was spared, so we continued living there. My mother was outraged to see what was happening. This was her country. Terrible changes were taking place in it before her eyes, and it seemed as if she could never feel comfortable or safe again. What if she had to flee? If, in the past, she had sometimes spoken in the abstract about the possibility of having to leave Egypt, she had never really believed it might one day come to pass. Exodus did not fit into her view of the future. Nor did living in another country, as an exile, where the language and customs were strange, and the future was uncertain.

7

London, Our Temporary Residence

*R*egardless of my mother's feelings, violent forces were on the move all around her family. Jews had been leaving Egypt in droves since the late 1940s. Now Jews were being attacked in Egypt, and by November of 1950, possibly fifty thousand—more than half of the total population of Jews in Egypt—had fled the country, most for new lives in Israel. Their bank accounts were blocked and many became paupers overnight.

My mother was worried about us, especially my older brother. "What's going to happen to Jean-Pierre? How are we going to educate him?" She believed that educating *me* was not necessary.

Her second worry was her mother. My grandmother did not have a passport. She could not leave the country. My mother feared that, when we left, the soldiers were going to throw her mother in the street. All the money we had, all of our belongings, would be confiscated. In fact, when the soldiers finally came for us, they did, indeed, leave my grandmother in the street. Only later were we relieved to learn that she had contacted other family members in Cairo, and Jewish friends had taken her in. An Arab family we did not know would be moving into my grandmother's home.

When the soldiers came, they did not really care that my mother was Jewish. All they cared about was that my father was British, and that he worked at Marconi.

On our last day in Cairo, the guards led us to a plane painted on the sides with the letters BOAC. I had no idea that they stood for British Overseas Airways Corporation, but I was thrilled at the prospect of flying in an airplane. My father appeared relieved that we were finally leaving, and so did his brothers and sister. But not my mother or brother; you would have thought they were being escorted to their graves. Paulette and Jean-Pierre were both pale and their expressions grim.

All ten of us Trigacis settled into our airplane seats. The authorities had ousted not only us, but also Tony's brother, Carlo, and his wife, Lydia; another brother, Gino, and his wife, Nena; and a sister, Alice, and her husband, Richard. All of the men except my uncle Carlo worked for Marconi. From Cairo, we all flew to Amsterdam, where we spent the night in a hotel. I had never even seen the inside of a hotel. Then we went on to London.

After we arrived in London, Alice and Richard went to stay with one of his cousins. Then a few months later, they moved to Bahrain, in the Persian Gulf.

Shell Oil, my uncle Carlo's employer, sent a car for him and his wife, Lydia. Carlo and Lydia spent several months at a very comfortable Shell guesthouse before moving on to South Africa.

Tony's three other sisters, married to Lebanese, felt safe in Egypt and had stayed behind.

After we landed at Heathrow Airport, we walked out of the main terminal and into the busy lobby. No one was there to greet us. Outside, under a slate-gray sky, we gathered like the lost souls that we had become as the cold air bit through our thin clothes. I was wearing a dress and a light wrap. We were without money and winter clothes. Who had needed winter coats in Egypt?

We had no place to go. Scrambling to find us shelter, my father located Eddie Darmanin. He had served in the army with my father in Egypt, and they shared a Maltese heritage. Eddie came to pick us up. My parents, Jean-Pierre and I, and Gino and his wife, Nena, piled into Eddie's little Hillman. It was just as well that we did not have luggage. Eddie and his wife, Lilly, said we could stay with them for a while.

"We can put you up for a few weeks but not much longer," Eddie told us. "Our house is too small."

My family stayed for thirteen months.

They had one bedroom for us—a stark space with one double bed and a closet. A window opened onto the front of the building. My brother and I slept on blankets on the floor. Our mother fell into a state of denial and depression. In part, she was grieving the loss of her country. The Darmanins did not like her much, and the feeling was mutual. The Darmanins were simple people, while my mother was haughty. She refused to go out. She hibernated in the room like a miserable bear in winter. The couple worked, and my father desperately sought a job—not just any job, but a position equivalent to his former one in Egypt. When he returned from job-hunting in the evening, he cooked, even though he was no good at it. My mother was not much help. Still in pain over all she had lost, mostly she cried. Eventually, she found friends from Egypt and took some comfort in them.

I was enrolled in public school, where I could not understand anything anybody said. I spoke primarily French, and some Arabic. I knew only a few words and phrases in English. No longer a good student, I was lost. I was labeled "retarded." In my school there was one black girl who became my friend. A white couple had adopted her, and so she felt like a stranger both in her family and at school. I was trying to be adopted by a new country but not succeeding very well. We both were outcasts, and we felt as if we had grown up before our time.

Noticing that I was miserable at school and learning nothing, my father put me in a Catholic school, where the nuns took the time to try to teach me English. I remained an anomaly, however, for almost everyone there was fair-skinned, red-haired and Irish, with names like Sullivan and O'Malley. In their midst, I was the brown-haired, dark-skinned, dark-eyed Jewish-Egyptian-Catholic with the unlikely name of Micheline Trigaci. None of the others had ever met a Brit with a name like that.

By the time school was out, I was still struggling with English.

Fortunately, from June through August of 1957, I attended a summer camp in Lyme Regis, in Dorset in southwestern England, where I learned the new language by playing games and interacting with people. I learned more than English during that time. For instance, in Egypt, the only trees I had ever seen were palm trees. But in England, I became acquainted with a variety of leafy-green trees with branches I could climb. I helped pay my way to camp by working on the property, picking fruit and tending animals—cows, pigs and goats which, like the leafy trees, I had never seen before. I did not really miss my parents while I was at camp. They were depressed, and at the Darmanins' house, I had felt as if I could not breathe.

After I left the summer camp, I began to feel much more comfortable in London. Back with the Darmanins, I shopped for groceries and left the house more often than I had before. I liked seeing the people in the streets and shops, and wondering who they were and what they did. I was especially struck by their mannerisms, so different from those of Egyptians. Everybody in London spoke quietly, and the customers asked, "May I, please?"

when they wanted something. In Cairo, people in the markets shouted, "Give me that!"

England also struck me as much more interesting and prosperous than Egypt. England did not have the terrible sandstorms that caused people to put wet towels under their doors to keep out the sand. Daily life seemed easier for most people in England, though not necessarily for the people I saw living in Eddie Darmanin's neighborhood, Balham. Balham was not prosperous at all. Hardly any of the damage it had sustained during World War II had been repaired, and many of the residents struggled to make ends meet.

I tried hard to adjust and I enjoyed some success, but my time in London was mostly difficult. I tried very hard to forget Arabic because I did not believe I could manage to speak three languages. In Egypt, we had spoken French and Arabic. When we went to England, my father and I made a pact that we would speak English to each other, an agreement we kept until the day he died. Everybody else in the family spoke French at home. I spoke French to my mother throughout her life, even though she eventually learned English.

8

Living in the Land of Babel

I am the only member of my multilingual family who failed to master more than two languages. Although French was our staple, my parents, brother, aunts, uncles and cousins were all proficient in a laundry list of languages. In addition to French, my father could slip smoothly in and out of Greek, Arabic, Italian and English. My brother mastered Spanish. Until my mother's memory started to fade, she was fluent in four languages.

I had plenty of opportunities to join the multilingual club. In first grade, we were taught to read and write, first in French, and by the middle of the year in English. In second grade, Arabic was added to our repertoire. By the time I was twelve and we were settled in London, I realized that, although I knew a smattering of three languages, I did not have a full command of any of them. I also began to notice a fuzziness in my family's linguistic picture. As recent exiles from Egypt, my family did not have a country we could call home, and now I could see that we had no mother tongue, either.

Listening to my father and his siblings speak a cacophony of languages made me suspect that knowing too many languages made it harder—not easier—to express ideas and emotions articulately. I wondered whether knowing many languages was truly an advantage. At the time, I would have been hard-pressed to explain my sentiments. Mine was an intuitive, gut reaction rather than insightful deliberation.

Over time, I grew to realize that I had been right, and that sometimes the more languages one spoke, the weaker the command of each one. Language influences and molds us. We read books, and we watch television shows and movies in our mother tongue. We are shaped by what we read and see. Without a native tongue, we are visitors in any number of cultures, but at home in none.

I began to realize that my parents, my brother, and members of my extended family, all boasting the same linguistic skills, were detached from the cultures of these languages. They looked on words as tools, more like kitchen utensils that could easily be substituted, one for another. If you could not find the spatula, a slotted spoon would work. If you did not know the right word in Italian, maybe you could find an equivalent in Greek, or in Arabic. In addition, you could not be taken to task for grammatical errors in any of the languages you spoke, since none of them was your native tongue. You did not feel the need to learn the more intricate and subtle rules of vocabulary and grammar. Because my family lived among others of a similar persuasion, they could switch back and forth and navigate this frequently choppy mélange with relative ease.

Particularly striking was their ability to switch languages, dependent upon the subject at hand.

"How can you tell a joke in English?" my father would ask rhetorically. "English is not a funny language."

My father claimed that jokes were funny only when told in Arabic, a language replete in subtleties unavailable in other tongues. When my mother got angry, she would switch to Arabic, my father to Greek. Living in Hong Kong as a teenager, I was often mortified when my father, angered by another driver's moves, would roll down the window and yell profanities in Greek—to the astonishment of the other driver who, more often than not, was Chinese. In my house, French was the language of everyday use, and English was reserved for discussions of business and money. Italian signaled conversations the children were not supposed to hear. Neither my brother nor I learned it.

In any given conversation, as the subject shifted, so did the language. As a teenager, when I invited girlfriends to lunch or dinner at home, I would plead with my parents to speak English, and English only. They would promise, but their good intentions rarely prevailed. I dreaded the look of surprise that would appear on friends' faces when, after a few minutes of polite conversation in English, one of my parents would suddenly start the switching game and the other would follow suit. I remember a lunch one Saturday when my father felt particularly stressed because the Chinese staff at the telegraph company where he worked was threatening to strike. I had invited my friend Annabel to lunch.

"It is abominable," my father said in English to my mother. "You don't understand, Paulette, how much we have done for the staff. After all that, to behave that way is disgraceful."

My mother disagreed vehemently. She thought that what was abominable were the attitudes of the colonial British administration. The subject was no longer business. It had veered into the emotional. So, of course, she switched to French.

"*Tu n'est pas raisonable, Tony. Tu ne sais même pas ce que tu raconte,*" my mother answered.

The conversation became heated, English was abandoned, and French became the language du jour.

"*Zeft*" (rubbish), my mother said in Arabic, annoyed at her failure to change my father's mind.

"I thought we were going to speak English," I pleaded.

"Oh, sorry, Miche," one of them replied.

But my protest was never of any use because the English respite never lasted long. I became known as the kid with the odd "foreign" parents.

Egypt had been home to my family for at least two generations, maybe more. About its own history, my family's collective memory was as fuzzy as its command of grammar and syntax. And among foreigners in Egypt, language indeterminacy ran rampant. Most of the resident foreign community in Egypt could trace their roots throughout the Mediterranean, Spain, and the former French colonies of North Africa. But they had roamed for so long, few could remember from where originally they had hailed. This was a community of true expatriates, of rootless émigrés who had traded stability for interesting, colorful lives.

When Gamal Abdel Nasser expelled émigrés from Egypt in 1956, the community scattered. Egypt's expatriate diaspora extended to every continent, including the United States. In London, my English was not good enough to enable me to understand my teachers, or to converse with my classmates. When I set about learning English properly, I became aware of my family's linguistic peculiarities and of their inability to master appropriate accents in any language. They spoke all languages with a generic foreign accent.

Learning to speak English properly, and with the right accent, became my goal. I decided to stop speaking other languages. My mother disagreed. "We are not going to speak English at home," she said in French. "I am not going to speak to my children in a foreign language. *Voilá. Oof. Quelle bêtise. Ca suffit ces bêtises.*"

But my more easygoing father wavered.

"*Comme tu veux, cherie,*" he told my mother. "The children need to learn English, but we'll do whatever you want. Whatever you think is best." But later he agreed to speak to me only in English. We made our English-only pact on January 1, 1957. He died forty years later, not having once broken our agreement.

Our household remained a Babel, but I focused entirely on mastery of English. I was fascinated by the multitudes of inflections and enunciations that I heard all around me. At my Catholic school, the Irish nuns spoke with a soft and pleasant lilt. In the streets of South London, the accents were raw and harsh. On the radio, I listened to the cultured and clipped speech of British Broadcasting Corporation announcers. At home, I learned vocabulary. Every evening, my father would pull out his dictionary and methodically select words, identifying twenty or perhaps thirty words in English that I would memorize. His pronunciation was not always reliable. He would put the emphasis on the wrong syllable, and when I showed off my new words at school the next day, I was often met by giggles or quizzical looks.

Jean-Pierre decided to learn only enough English to get by. No more. Fifty years later, despite having earned a degree from the University of London and having lived most of his life in English-speaking countries, he continues to speak English with a heavy, somewhat unidentifiable foreign accent.

By the time we moved to Hong Kong for the first time in 1957, my English had improved but I was still not as fluent as I wanted to be. In Hong Kong, I discovered the British Council. Located on the second floor of the stately, downtown Gloucester Building, the library was free. So far, my exposure to books had been very limited. No one in my family read books for either information or enjoyment, although my father put great faith in his dictionary and later in his books about the game of bridge. I had not known public libraries existed. Our school library in London had been a dark, musty room packed with classics and religious texts. I never saw anyone go into it.

The British Council Library became my favorite haunt. I rode the bus there every Saturday morning and spent hours choosing the books I would take home. At first, I read novels. Then I read short stories. I loved Somerset Maugham. I was fascinated by Doris Lessing's African stories and later her tomes on women. I read love stories and I read books I did not understand. Anais Nin and Ayn Rand were particularly mysterious and confusing. I read *Atlas Shrugged* without having any idea what it was about. Then I discovered a bookshelf of plays—contemporary scripts by such playwrights as Noel Coward. I read them aloud in the privacy of my bedroom. The more I read, the more comfortable I became with the English language, its sounds and its usage.

By the end of our first year in Hong Kong, my English was fluent. The more I read and wrote, the more I grew to realize the validity of my early decision. In order to appreciate a language, to savor its literature, and to express yourself both orally and on paper, you must have a strong sense of that tongue, a familiarity with its nuances, an intrinsic feeling for its structures and sounds, and a sense of the culture that it both shapes and reflects. I am sure there are some particularly talented people who may be able to attain this level of fluency in more than one or two languages. But I would suggest that they are the exceptions.

For most of us, one language is all we can master. Becoming conversant in other languages is an advantage. But lacking a dominant language, and an understanding of the cultural mores it conveys, is most definitely a deficit.

9

Unsettled in London
1957

*I*n the fall of 1957, following the summer camp in Lyme Regis, I went back to Catholic school knowing so much more English that I was a far better student than I had been the year before. My mother, however, did not adjust nearly as well to London. Even after she found some Egyptian friends and quit hibernating, she kept asking, "Where do I go, what do I do? I don't know how to talk to people." She expected my father to take care of her. Many women of her generation were like that.

I felt differently about the world. I would say, "I'm going to be a newspaper reporter," and she would say, "Don't even say such words." She would tell me, "Women don't work." My mother never even learned to drive. She never wrote a check. She said, "How will you marry a rich man if you're always reading a newspaper?"

Family was my mother's highest priority in life, and the expulsion from Cairo that scattered her kin to distant lands created in her a severe sense of traumatic displacement. She had left her mother behind. Her two sisters, Georgette and Raymonde, had fled to Australia with their families. Paulette was brokenhearted. She missed them all terribly. Owing to my father's job with Marconi, we had enjoyed a free telephone back home in Cairo. Paulette had phoned her sisters every day. Now this contact was no longer possible. Years would pass before Paulette had enough money to visit her sisters in Australia.

We had been a close family. Paulette's sister Georgette, or Joujou as we called her, had no children. Raymonde had two, Philippe and Daniele. Daniele, who is seven days younger than I, is a close friend of mine as well as a cousin. Before we left Cairo, Daniele and I made a pact never to lose touch with each other. Even then, like my mother, I had a strange fear that, despite our pledge, it was possible to be swept away from relatives and all that I knew and loved. I would soon understand what it was like to be without a country.

Although my father had been a loyal employee at the British-owned Marconi Cable & Wireless in Cairo, the British government did nothing to help us in London. My father initially knew little English, but he went to Marconi and said, "I've got to have a job." Everything they offered him was low-level employment. That did not interest him. He went a whole year without a job, but as things turned out he was right to hold his ground.

The Darmanins, meanwhile, grew tired of putting us up. Lilly Darmanin was sick of my mother's behavior, and of seventeen-year-old Jean-Pierre, who sat in a corner and never talked to anybody. Inheriting more of my father's disposition, I tried to make the best of this unhappy situation and found things to enjoy amid all these varied experiences. We had no money, but my father faithfully gave my brother and me enough to take the bus to school—about two pennies each for our roundtrip fare. My brother saved his pennies and rose an hour early to walk to school. I began to suspect that he had some kind of a plan.

I tried to like it, but life in London never became the exciting adventure I had anticipated. Our living conditions were miserable. Gone were Cairo's bright sunlight and big sky, the panoramic views from our balcony. London was cold, damp and dreary. The gravity of our new reality had begun to seep into my mind two days after my twelfth birthday. I felt I had been abruptly vaulted out of childhood and into a foreign world of grown-up worries, a world in which we were powerless. True, I had the gift of an all-important British passport, but what had it gotten me? I was in Balham, not in the London of glittery shops, Parliament buildings and Big Ben that I had dreamed about seeing one day.

My parents continued to be unhappy in London as well, and they fought a lot. My mother had almost decided that Australia would not be so bad after all. At least she would be close to her sisters. We stayed with the Darmanins in England until December 15, 1957, when my father finally received a job offer with Cable and Wireless, the British phone company. They offered him a chance to go to Hong Kong, Saskatchewan, or South America.

When my mother learned of this, she said, "I don't go to places I can't pronounce the names of, and I heard it snows in Canada."

Tony said they told him he could stay forever in Hong Kong if he liked it. Otherwise, he would have to move every three years. My father chose Hong Kong.

"But where is Hong Kong?" my mother would ask.

Because I felt I would never truly be at home or accepted in England or anywhere else, I liked the idea of moving every three years. Tony said that, instead, we would be moving to a bigger house every three years. I had to be satisfied with that.

Jean-Pierre, now eighteen, balked at the idea of moving. To my mother's dismay, he announced that he would stay behind in London, where his life had already assumed a direction my parents would abhor when they learned of it.

Meanwhile, Paulette continued to insist, "I am not going to live in China."

"It's not China," my father repeated, patiently at first, and later in tense tones, his voice rising. "It is a British colony." Then he would add almost to himself, with a shudder, "Just think of what would have happened if the children had not had passports."

10

My Unconventional Brother Jean-Pierre

*M*y brother and I had learned to swim in an Olympic-sized pool at the Guezzirah Sporting Club on the outskirts of Cairo. It was a beautiful pool surrounded by impeccably manicured lawns. Our father never learned to swim. He grew up in the flat, arid Egyptian countryside, miles away from the sea. The ocean terrified him, and even the calm water that filled swimming pools made him anxious. When he took us to the country club, he would walk along the sides of the pool, never taking his eyes off us. My mother, who could swim, usually lay on a lounge chair near the pool and kept an eye on us while chatting to her friends.

When Jean-Pierre was about ten, he decided to learn to swim underwater. To our father's chagrin, Jean-Pierre became very good at it. In one of my earliest memories of my father, I see him pacing along the sides of the pool, back and forth, his arms behind his back, sweat pouring off his bald head, as Jean-Pierre navigates the depths of the pool, up and down, over and over again. The boy never seemed to grow tired of it.

"Are you all right?" our father would ask, as he wrapped his son, finally emerged and trembling from the cold water, in a towel. "Are you sure you are all right?" Our father could not understand why Jean-Pierre would, of his own volition, dive to the bottom of the pool and stay there for extended periods of time.

"You don't have to do it again," he would say. "We've seen that you can do it."

With Jean-Pierre on dry land, our father's sweating abated, and he regained his composure. Our father shared none of my brother's enthusiasm for water sports. Much more conventionally, Tony loved soccer and enjoyed a game of tennis. Jean-Pierre, however, shunned everything that he saw as conventional. Second only to his passion for underwater swimming was his attraction to fencing, yet another activity that made my father uncomfortable. In fact, just about everything Jean-Pierre chose to do either confused or troubled Tony.

This discomfort and confusion would perhaps have been less had our lives been more stable. These feelings of rootlessness may have had something to do with the fact that Jean-Pierre and I stopped calling our parents by the conventional names of "Mother" and "Father." Instead, in a kind of ritual renaming that possibly signified our loss of the past, we chose to begin calling our parents by their first names.

Nearly fifty years after leaving Egypt, my brother remains a displaced person whose behavior suggests that he feels truly at home with no one and nowhere. Jean-Pierre is my only sibling. Born in 1939, he is five years my senior. I can only imagine the joy that spread through my Sephardic family when my mother brought a first-born son into the world. My maternal grandfather had three daughters; my mother was the eldest. His brother also had three daughters. My grandfather thought it embarrassing, if not downright humiliating, to have so many girls in the family. As a very young girl, I remember hearing my grandfather mutter about the difficulty of finding husbands for so many girls. When my mother became the first of the six girls to bear a son, the birth was cause for great celebration. My parents lived with my maternal grandparents at the time. When they brought Jean-Pierre home from the hospital, our grandparents were so eager to make him comfortable that they moved permanently out of their own bedroom, the largest in the apartment, into a smaller one. The new baby boy would grow up in the best, biggest, and brightest room available.

Perhaps because he was male, perhaps because the family's future was so tenuous, everyone indulged all of Jean-Pierre's whims. By the time he was eight, my parents had hired a young Sudanese servant whose job it was to care for, feed and entertain Jean-Pierre. For many months, until the neighbors complained, Jean-Pierre chose to eat his meals in the tiny elevator of our building. It was a French contraption with a large outside metal door over wooden interior doors, and inside were a tiny bench and a mirror. Young Jean-Pierre sat on the bench while the Sudanese boy squatted, plate and spoon in hand, feeding my brother, as the elevator crawled and creaked up and down, ascending and descending repeatedly from the ground floor to the sixth floor where we lived. I have pictures of my brother from those days. He was a good-looking child, despite the clothes my mother chose for him: old-fashioned smocks, embroidered shirts and short pants, outdated long before the 1940s when the photos were taken.

Jean-Pierre and I never talk about our childhood. We rarely even exchange an anecdote, recall an event, or recount an incident. Even though we grew up in the same home and we both have pleasant memories of our childhood, we do not seem to have any joint reminiscences. We went to different schools and led very separate lives. We both went to the club and to the pool, often after school, and nearly always on weekends, but we must have gone our own ways most of the time. Still, I find it odd that we don't revisit the shared part of our past together.

I think Jean-Pierre learned early in life—certainly much earlier than I did—that he could carve his own path and that my parents were not infallible. I thought for a long time that Jean-Pierre was impervious to other people's opinions, but I was wrong. While I tried to please and to blend in, he strove to shock and to stand out. We both wanted approval, but we went about seeking it in different ways. He wanted to be seen as daring and unusual.

His self-dramatizations began early, and one of the most memorable ones concerned religion. Jean-Pierre and I were raised Catholic. On Sunday mornings, my aunt Alice, my father's older sister, would collect us and take us to mass. Aunt Alice also took us both to catechism classes. However, around the age of ten, having received his first communion and gone through confirmation, Jean-Pierre decided to renounce religion. He made his announcement at dinner on a Friday night, when the Jewish side of my family had gathered for a Shabbat meal.

"I am going to become an atheist," he said.

"Shush," my mother said quickly, her face turning red. "We'll talk about this later."

I am not sure he even knew what "atheist" meant. I certainly did not, although I could guess that it was something bad. Everyone looked stunned and began talking at the same time, trying to drown out any more of Jean-Pierre's proclamations. The conversation continued as if nothing had happened. No one ever talked about it again, at least not in front of me, but Jean-Pierre never again went to mass.

This incident, though no one knew it at the time, revealed much about the man this strong-willed little boy would become. During the time following our departure from Egypt, while we were living in London for a year, my eighteen-year-old brother began to keep more and more to himself. When Tony announced he had found a job in Hong Kong, my parents and I left London, but Jean-Pierre stayed behind to go to university, where he had decided to study geology. He lived with friends he had made over the past months while he had been saving his bus fare. Although he wrote regularly to my parents, and occasionally telephoned them, I had no contact at all with him for the next three years until I returned to London at age sixteen. He seemed like a stranger when I saw him again.

11

Life in Hong Kong

1957-1999

*A*fter a month at sea, the *SS Corfu* sailed into Hong Kong's harbor early in the morning on December 15, 1957, carrying my parents and me to yet another destination. Leaving my brother behind was devastating to my mother. Even so, she was much happier in Hong Kong. The weather was more to her liking, and she could live in better style. In our new home, we had three bedrooms, two bathrooms, and a balcony overlooking the harbor and, best of all for my mother, a servant once again. Soon my parents were making friends, especially among the French from the French consulate.

The British government furnished our apartment, but over time my mother bought Chinese furnishings and accent pieces to put her own stamp on the home. The longer we stayed, the more stylish the house looked. That is how she dealt with exile. She tried to make a domestic space of her own, and to make it pretty. When my parents eventually left Hong Kong twenty years later, in 1977, they took all of the Chinese furniture and accessories my mother had acquired back to London with them.

Aboard the *SS Corfu*, my parents and I were among the many passengers who lined the decks and craned our necks to get a first glimpse of the city that was to be our new home. To one side of the harbor, we saw mountains, their peaks covered in fog, and along the waterside, low, white, colonial-style buildings with large verandas. Across the mile-long stretch of harbor, in the adjoining town of Kowloon, a six-story, red-brick clock tower rose above a railway station. Low buildings, docks, and warehouses dotted the flat landscape. The morning was cool and the air misty. All three of us had the silent but sinking sensation of having arrived at a remote outpost more suitable as the scene of a quaint Chinese watercolor than as a town we could call home.

It struck me, as it must have struck my parents, that we were exiles and would have very little in common with people in this new place. It would be as strange to us as London had been. Yet, very quickly, I fell in love with Hong Kong, and I began to find it fascinating. I went to school with a group of people who respected me, and I soon learned enough Chinese to go to the market. The English-language school I attended was a good one. Everybody considered my family the "in" people. It was a school for the children of British government employees. I must have picked up something from the generally enterprising atmosphere of Hong Kong because, for the first time in a long while, I began to feel as if I had the opportunity to excel, to go places. I was very determined to do well. I liked to read and consumed works of literature. I did not join clubs or play sports, but I had friends and dated four or five different boys, although none seriously. They came to the house and we went to the beach.

The Hong Kong that greeted us in 1957 was packed with refugees from China, but these were not the type of migrants who were most familiar to me. I was well acquainted with people of broken spirits, people forced out of their homes by political upheaval, people who had resigned themselves to accepting that the best years of their lives were behind them and who tended to live in the past.

Most of the two-and-a-half-million people who had settled in Hong Kong by 1957 had left their homes in China at the onset of the Communist Revolution, eight years earlier. Unlike the expatriates I had known so far, these Chinese people were energetic and confident. They were determined to devote their lives to the accumulation of wealth. They had become the embodiment of modern refugees—displaced men and women seeking an economic haven, rather than merely fleeing political or social persecution. I was inspired by their example, and for the first time began to feel as though living in exile need not be a reason for despair.

The original Chinese settlers of Hong Kong first threw their lot in with the British in 1841 when Britain colonized their island, capturing it as their prize for having prevailed over the Chinese during the first Opium War. In 1898, when negotiating the end of the second Opium War, the British Crown Colony of Hong Kong was granted a ninety-nine-year lease on additional territory in the adjoining New Territories. Throughout the nineteenth century, Hong Kong was a thinly populated outpost whose raison d'être was limited to making money from the opium trade. Hong Kong's leaders had little interest in spreading evangelical principles or furthering the imperial ambitions that prevailed among powerful colonial leaders in Whitehall. Consider James Matheson, a leading merchant whose trading company was to become the largest opium dealer in Hong Kong. In response to critics and religious entities who argued strongly against opium on ethical grounds, Matheson said: "We have every respect for persons entertaining strict religious principles, but we fear that very godly people are not suited to the drug trade."[1]

Hong Kong's commercial scope of interest and population grew slowly, and it was not until World War II and the subsequent Communist Revolution in China that Hong Kong truly came into its own. By 1948, refugees had begun streaming into Hong Kong, at first legally and in later years risking their lives to enter the colony. They all wanted a piece of the golden halo that was reputed to hang over the British territory. Many of these men and women arrived in Hong Kong without any possessions whatsoever. Some had been successful, wealthy entrepreneurs. Others were middle-class professionals. Still others were manual laborers, fishermen, and farmers. Some either had money already, or possessed the wherewithal to make it. I considered my father one of the latter.

After 1948, at first, refugees often lived in communities of shacks that soon covered mile upon mile of hillsides—communities that were frequently devastated by fires and by the mudslides that followed typhoons. Within two decades, many of these same refugees became Hong Kong's business and professional elite.

The refugees were mostly Chinese, but there was a generous sprinkling of people from other parts of the world—from cultures as diverse as India and Iran, Britain and Australia. They came in search of money, but they were also hungry for color and culture, for sunshine and adventure, and for the opportunity to move outside their own societies' rigid constraints. The pursuit of money, however, and the opportunity to make it, regardless of ethnicity or family connections, was the language they had in common. And if life could be interesting and out of the ordinary as well, so much the better. My family and I felt that opportunity was within our grasp in Hong Kong; something we had not felt in London.

And opportunities abounded. I finished secondary school in Hong Kong at age seventeen in July, 1962, and a few days later I walked into the newsroom of the *Hong Kong Standard*, looking for a job. I knew nothing about journalism, but I was undeterred. The paper was owned by a Chinese family and run by a group of Australians who had known one another in Sydney. They were a rough bunch of uncouth and adventurous of young men. The only woman in the news operation was Mildred Wong, a middle-aged Shanghainese who always wore high-collared silk cheongsams, even at the height of the summer. She never seemed to perspire, despite the heat, the humidity, the absence of air conditioning in the building, and the proximity of the newsroom to the lead presses.

The smoky, sweltering newsroom became my home for the next year. I learned to smoke, to drink beer and Scotch, to report and write news stories. The sub-editors, or "subs," as we called them, taught me to write by refusing to rewrite my stories. They would make me write and rewrite, over and again, until I got the hang of it—and until I was nearly in tears.

Nothing that I have seen or experienced since leaving Hong Kong can compare to the excitement, the diversity, and the interest that Hong Kong held for me in those days. It has often been said that, for those willing to take chances, Hong Kong opened the door to many a triumphant venture. This was certainly true of one of my editors in Hong Kong. An Indian from the former colony of Goa, A. V. Pandit had grown disenchanted with the heavy hand of Portuguese occupiers. In Hong Kong, he launched a business magazine and soon was publishing more than a dozen titles that were distributed throughout Southeast Asia.

One of the wealthiest families in Hong Kong was the Kadoories. Sephardic Jews of Iranian descent, they had immigrated first to China, where they became property and business owners, and later to Hong Kong, where they acquired utilities, hotels and industries. The family eventually became the largest benefactor of the Shanghai Art Museum built in the 1970s, a few miles away from the mansion that they once had owned, and that the Chinese government had confiscated in 1949.

Hong Kong's ranks of refugees also included a large contingent of Russian Jews who traced their ancestors to the Eastern Russian city of Vladivostok. Fleeing the pogroms against Jews in World War I, they had settled in the thriving western Chinese city of Harbin. The post-World War I economic boom in Shanghai had encouraged many of them to move once more. The Sino-Japanese War began in 1937. In 1942 the Japanese rounded up Shanghai's Jews and interned them in camps for the duration of the war. Surprisingly, the Japanese ignored demands by the Nazi government that the Jews be annihilated. Most survived the war but, by 1948, with the Communist Revolution gathering force in China, the Russian Jews were displaced once more, this time settling in Hong Kong. The Zirinskys, one of the better-known Russian families in Hong Kong, ran an export-import business, helped found a Jewish community center and also acted as honorary representatives of Israel.

In the economically depressed Britain of the 1950s, the colonies remained the best opportunity for the country's ambitious, imaginative and restless men and women. Seducing many a young Englishman to set out on an adventure in Hong Kong were images of deep-red sunsets, lush-green hills rising from white-sandy beaches, exotic junks sailing through the picturesque Hong Kong harbor, and white-coated waiters—on yachts or on verandas of lavish apartment buildings—serving tall drinks to *gweilos* (literally, "ghost fellows," a term used in Hong Kong to refer to Westerners). Fresh out of Cambridge with a degree in history, one of my acquaintances, David Perkins, could have looked for a job in Britain, but Hong Kong had more to offer. Unless you were born into the right family, well-paid employment in England was scarce, as my father had learned. And life in Britain was unlikely to have the luster that Hong Kong promised. Perkins came to Hong Kong, where he went to work for Radio Hong Kong and quickly became a well-paid local celebrity.

Australians were less tempted by Hong Kong's scenic beauty. They were drawn instead by the mix of cultures and by the colony's exotic atmosphere, so different from that of Australia. Mike Foote, for instance, did not think twice when he was offered a job with an advertising agency in Hong Kong. He jumped at the opportunity to make money, to live in a colorfully diverse city, and to leave behind Melbourne's bland, constricted way of life.

Such success stories, and there were hundreds, belonged to those who were able almost intuitively to perceive opportunities and to take risks—people such as Li Ka-Shing, who in 1950 was able to recognize a demand in the United States for plastic flowers and who developed his tiny business into one of the world's largest empires, and Sir Y. K. Pao, who started out in the same period and was able to create a shipping empire unmatched in the world, both in size and profitability. Multimillionaires proliferated in Hong Kong, all self-made, all owing their success to their acuity, courage, and determination. They made money in hula-hoops, clothing, textiles, electronics, real estate, and commercial shipping, and they owed their success to the swiftness with which they took advantage of breaks. All of them—Chinese, Russians, Indians, Iranians, Australians and Brits—came looking for alternatives to what was available to them at home and for the opportunity to use their imagination and ingenuity to amass, if not fortunes, at least sufficient assets. Together, they all built in Hong Kong a city-state unparalleled in the world. They converted the rocky, barren island into an exhilarating, energetic, and economically thriving metropolis. An island once dominated by primitive fishing villages and shantytowns became one of the world's most elegant and sophisticated cities, an international trade and financial center, and the hub of finance and culture in Southeast Asia.

It was against that backdrop that we arrived, ready to launch our new lives but not fully understanding how thoroughly different this colony was from the rest of the British Empire. The discussion about my passport did not come up this time, and it would be years before I would understand the full significance of its origins, and of what my father had done to obtain it.

Hong Kong was a crowded and noisy city that thrived on speed and movement, unlike the "old world" we had just left. In only a few decades, Hong Kong had shed all vestiges of its beginnings as a haven for refugees. The memories of displacement, the anxiety of exile, the apprehension of an untested new land had all faded. You did not have to be educated or rich to play the game of making it in Hong Kong.

Years later, when my first husband and I lived in the city, the maid we employed to look after our children was barely literate. She often spent a considerable amount of time every morning in animated telephone conversations. I eventually discovered that she was buying stocks and trading currencies. She could not read a newspaper headline, but she knew the daily fluctuations in the yuan and the yen, the Australian and the American dollars. I have no doubt that her assets were considerably larger than ours were. What makes her noteworthy is that she was not an anomaly.

The British and Hong Kong Chinese had come to a mutual understanding after World War II. The British would run Hong Kong. They would provide an efficient police force, build an airport, maintain roads, keep the air and water clean, collect as few taxes as possible, and otherwise stay out of the way. The Chinese would not get involved in managing Hong Kong, nor would they make any political moves that could incense the giant across the border. In return, they would be left to their own devices, free to make as much money as they pleased, with as few obstacles as possible in their way. The agreement served everyone well.

By the mid-1960s, Hong Kong's harbor was a frenzy of activity. Hong Kong was teeming with financiers and investment bankers, realtors and architects, and Kowloon was dotted with high-rise industrial buildings, each floor humming with machinery, and each factory feeding specialty stores in Europe and America.

Hong Kong's progress, however, had not been smooth. There were many rough spots when the economic émigrés thought twice about their gamble, and when many wondered whether immigrating to the United States would have been the sounder, safer move. The American embargo on goods from China after the Korean War cast a pall over Hong Kong, which relied heavily on the entrepôt trade. International textile agreements limited Hong Kong's exports and threatened to strangle its future. In the mid-1970s, the Hong Kong Stock Market saw values fall overnight at an alarming and precipitous rate, wiping out hundreds of investors and giving rise to questions about management and integrity. Years of droughts tempered the most optimistic soul. Other natural disasters added to the tension. In the aftermath of a typhoon in 1972, for example, a luxury high-rise apartment building midway up the Peak, in an area known as the Mid-Levels, slipped into an avalanche of mud, and more than one hundred residents were killed.

The defining moment, however, was the Cultural Revolution. The foreign and Chinese communities had kept largely to themselves until 1967, when the Cultural Revolution in China spilled across the border to Hong Kong and Red Guards marched down the main thoroughfares playing patriotic hymns to Chairman Mao. Hong Kong was unnerved. The stock market faltered, real estate values fell sharply, wealthy families shipped their valuables out of the colony, and money began to flow out of Hong Kong. But despite its frayed nerves, Hong Kong kept its cool. The British national anthem was piped into main streets to drown out Red Guards' propaganda. All of Hong Kong gritted its teeth and acted as though nothing untoward were happening. In the end, the Red Guards retreated, and although Hong Kong breathed a sigh of relief, the summer of 1967 served to remind Hong Kong of its precarious status and vulnerability.

It was a lesson my father never forgot.

The foreign and Chinese communities seemed to grow closer after the summer of 1967. The venerable Hong Kong Club began accepting Chinese members. British companies that had required their British employees to ask for permission before marrying a Chinese rescinded that policy, and there was a striking increase in the number of Chinese civil servants who were promoted within the Hong Kong government. Hearing a *gweilo* speak Cantonese was not commonplace, but it was no longer as surprising as it would have been a decade earlier. The rules of engagement had not changed—the British remained in charge of the administration and the Chinese ran the colony's economy—but the fine line between the British colonials and the financial émigrés had disappeared. Whether a Brit, a Chinese, an Indian, or an Australian, if you called Hong Kong home, Hong Kong belonged to you.

By the early 1970s, Hong Kong had developed an elegance that put ritzy European and American cities to shame, a brash, lavish lifestyle that made the most nouveau riche Texan or Californian blush; a self-confidence that encouraged and enabled many to succeed; and a zest for living and enjoying life to its limits. It was a way of life that was not only anathema to the Chinese across the border but also sometimes a little too rich and excessive for many Westerners. Hong Kong boasted more Rolls Royces per capita than any city in the world, and its residents were the world's largest consumers of fine French cognac. Despite the warm climate, fur stores did a thriving business. Women were bejeweled in diamonds and other glittering stones. Chinese tycoons were pictured in glossy magazines showing off their palatial mansions and yachts. On a typical Saturday afternoon, Hong Kong's high rollers spent more than $200 million gambling at the horse races. If you had it, you flaunted it. Wealthy Chinese *tai-tais* (wealthy Chinese wives) would spread their gowns and jewels in strategic parts of their homes for their guests to admire. Asking people how much they had paid for a purchase was polite because it gave them the opening to boast of their wealth and the vast sums they could afford to spend.

The Chinese worship their ancestors and traditionally burn food offerings to the gods in the hopes that the spirits of their ancestors will be well fed. To play it safe, the Hong Kong Chinese would burn some fake paper money as well—you never knew, money could come in handy, even in the afterlife.

The people of Hong Kong loved having money, making money, and spending money. Time was money, and there was no time to lose.

Hong Kong was nonstop noise. The noise gave rise to a nervous exhilaration. People moved quickly, they talked rapidly, they made decisions swiftly, and they expected everyone else to keep pace. Impatience hung in the air. Construction projects in Hong Kong were routinely completed at a record pace. Crews building the seventy-eight-story Central Plaza, for example, were proud to shave a day off Hong Kong's previous record of adding one story every four days.

Tony's natural optimism had found a place to flourish. His dreams of prosperity seemed possible after the dreary life we had known in London. Part of the key to making it in Hong Kong was being the first with the idea and the first to market it. But it was also adopting the attitude that everything was possible and that there was nothing that could not be accomplished. There was promise for the middle class as well. And the children of fishermen and farmers, maids and coolies went to school. In the barest of housing estates, on fishing boats and in crowded apartment buildings, rows upon rows of children would sit at makeshift tables and desks in the dusk of the evening, practicing their calligraphy and doing their sums.

Alice Yip, a good example of the upwardly mobile, is the daughter of refugees from Kwangtung, China, who worked as coolies and maids. Her parents were illiterate, but Alice graduated from a teacher's training college in Hong Kong. She teaches in a private Roman Catholic school. She was one of thousands who were offered an opportunity, who grasped it, and who now wonders what will be in the offing for her own children.

In 1997, this life in Hong Kong came to an abrupt and dreaded halt. The British acquiesced to China's claims on her lost territory. Gloomy and unimaginative Communist elders in China felt that Hong Kong had enjoyed life far too much, had enjoyed an excessive amount of glamour and glitz, intellect and intelligence. It was time to pull in the reins. Without consulting the people of Hong Kong, Britain had agreed to return to China the home these émigrés had created. The political dogma and economic inflexibility that plagued China were now threatening the laissez-faire creed that had come to give Hong Kong its luster. Displacement was in the cards once again for thousands of Hong Kong's citizens, who realized with dismay that they must move on. The question was where to go, when to go, for how long to stay put, and how to hedge their bets.

In the afternoon of June 30, 1997, members of the British royalty sailed into Hong Kong harbor. Charles, Prince of Wales, stood with Chinese officials for the handover ceremonies beginning at 11:30 p.m. Forty-five minutes later, Prince Charles and Hong Kong ex-governor Chris Patten, with his family, bid the citizens of Hong Kong farewell. They boarded Her Majesty's yacht, *Britannia*, and sailed to the Philippines. British sovereignty of Hong Kong had been officially transferred from the United Kingdom to the People's Republic of China.

The grand way of life of the colonials and the displaced inhabitants came to an end. The party was officially over.

Today, more than seven million residents of Hong Kong find themselves footloose once more. The British have gone, a temporary Chinese government has been installed, and the economic gains that once made the Hong Kong community so proud are disappearing. The abundant opportunities have diminished, and their lives are hanging in limbo. The people of Hong Kong must once again devise a game plan for their future. They must decide whether to stay in a city whose economic prospects have been severely curtailed and whose administration is now in the hands of political ideologues.

Displaced, rather than live in the new Hong Kong, the Brits and the Australians have left, along with my own family. Many have settled in France and Italy, in Malta and Portugal, where they can perhaps re-create at least some of the leisure and luxury they enjoyed in colonial Hong Kong. People like the Perkins and the Footes no longer think of London or Melbourne as their home; they don't think of anywhere as their home. Many of the Russian Jews have settled in London and Sydney. Jacob Zirinsky, the Zirinsky family's youngest child who, like his own children, was born in Hong Kong, is trying to find a new toehold in Sydney.

Many of the Chinese will toy with leaving but will stay in Hong Kong, where they can live safely but where they risk seeing all their hard work dismantled as the former colony's economic shine dulls. Perhaps the greatest contribution the economic émigrés made in Hong Kong was the creation of a middle class. But that middle class is now struggling the hardest because it has expectations that are unlikely to materialize. A new home is most elusive for this group.

Some of the Hong Kong Chinese will settle in a Western city— the likes of Vancouver or Sydney, both already teeming with people from Hong Kong. Perhaps they can re-create some of the magic that occurred in Hong Kong, where the blending of East and West, the combination of an efficient British government and a resourceful Chinese population, brought out the best in both. Or they can hedge their bets by obtaining a visa to a Western nation, tucking it away in a safe deposit box, while keeping, at least for a while, one foot in Hong Kong.

The conventional refugee stays home as long as possible and, when forced to leave, mourns the land he left behind. My family knows what it is like to grieve for a homeland that was lost. Some of us have suffered more than others because of that loss.

But the new breed of economic émigrés shows surprisingly little sentimentality toward their surroundings. The people of Hong Kong are in mourning, but the object of their grief is not the spectacular harbor or the steep, rocky hills. It is not the soft romantic mist that enveloped The Peak, either, or the typhoons that produced terrifying and electrifying light shows. They mourn a way of life that cannot be re-created; they long for the city that valued the pursuit of imagination, intuition and creativity, and they yearn for the environment that was conducive to the unfettered pursuit of wealth.

Columnist Thomas Friedman put it very well when he wrote in *The New York Times*: "Hong Kong's return to China is not just a slice of the West being given back to the East; it is a slice of the future being given back to the past."

I visited Hong Kong in 1999, two years after the handover to China. The contrast between the new and old was striking. The Chinese administration had already watered down the environmental rules the British had enforced. Hong Kong's air was now as dirty as the air in Beijing, which ranks among the most polluted cities in the world. Juxtaposed with this disappointing glimpse of the future was an inspiring scene from the past. The year before the British left, Hong Kong had conceived an idea that perfectly symbolized its ingenuity.

The eastern part of the island is both hilly and heavily populated. Commuters to the business district walk down the aptly named Ladder Street, which is composed of about two miles of stone steps, to get to work in the morning, and they climb up the same stairs in the evening. The walk to work is pleasant, but the climb home is rigorous. The roads, however, are too narrow and congested to accommodate more buses or cars. The solution? An escalator. In the morning, the electric contraption is set to go down, and in the evening, its course is reversed. Hong Kong is the only city where commuters pay a toll and ride an escalator to work. The escalator has come to symbolize Hong Kong's rapid advancement and its more recent reversal.

My parents lived in Hong Kong from 1957 until 1977, when Tony retired. While they were there, my father enjoyed a robust social life in this exciting city on the move. He went out to lunch and dinner with people. My parents became more refined and, unlike the city itself, quieter the longer they remained there. At the core, my father never really changed, though. He woke up happy, and he went to bed happy. He loved to come home from work and sit on the balcony with a drink—though he was never a big drinker—and gaze out at the boats on the harbor. He loved the Hong Kong environment. Later, back in England, I think he missed it.

Outside of his family, the two most important things in Tony's life were his job and the game of bridge. He developed quite a reputation in Hong Kong for his skill at bridge. He was the only one in my family who loved the game. I hate to play cards, and Jean-Pierre refused for some reason to play with him. My mother would not play either, because she said my father was too addicted to card games. They sometimes argued over this.

Still, Tony was so adept at bridge that he started to enter tournaments in Asia. I do not think he played for money, and I do not think that the games were televised. But his wins were written up in the *South China Morning Post*, and he was definitely known among card players throughout Asia and England.

Back in London, in his retirement, Tony and a friend played bridge almost every day. They played in the big tournaments and often ranked in the top ten. When Tony was nearly eighty-six, his friend had a fatal heart attack. My father never played bridge after that, and only about three months later, on June 1, 1997, he too passed away.

My parents might have stayed in Hong Kong even beyond 1977, but all their friends had begun retiring to England. Besides this, my father had begun to suffer a series of heart attacks. Hong Kong was becoming a more expensive place to live, and despite its increasing sophistication, it lacked good medical facilities. Most significantly, perhaps, the politics were turning ugly. My father repeated that he did not want to be a Brit in Hong Kong if it became Chinese. "I hope I die before they take it over." His wish was granted. He died a month before China reclaimed Hong Kong. He had been disturbed about the impending takeover. Everything he had known for so many years—the British telegraph company, the phone company—became Chinese-owned. He had seen all of it coming and wanted no part of it.

12

Back to London
1960-1961

I stayed in Hong Kong with my parents for two-and-a-half years, from 1958 until 1960. When I was sixteen, I returned to England for a school year, alone, while my parents took nine months off to see more of the world. They traveled by ship to San Francisco, New York, England and Australia.

In Hong Kong, I boarded a flight to England unescorted. When my plane stopped in India during a layover, I left the airport to see some of this country that I had flown over more than once. I ended up hitchhiking around India solo and then across Europe, taking in as much scenery as I could. Needless to say, when my parents got word that I had not arrived in London as expected, they were, in British understatement terms, not thrilled.

I eventually arrived at Mrs. Ada's London rooming house, my previously arranged home away from Hong Kong. It was run by a woman everyone called Mrs. Ada. I never heard anyone mention her first name. She was born in Manchester, but she had known my parents when they had all lived in Egypt.

Mrs. Ada had left Cairo when her husband died, and returned to England with her three daughters. Her home was gorgeous but uncomfortable, with twelve bedrooms and only one bathroom. She starved and froze her boarders. She used only tiny space heaters to warm the enormous house. Hungry, cold, and very lonely, I was far too young at age sixteen to be on my own in the world in such a depressing situation. Jean-Pierre had probably been told to look after me, but he was too involved in his own affairs and only stepped up to help me if I had a major problem.

I saw my brother about once a month, even though I wished for more contact. I never had enough money. My parents gave me £10 a month, and £8 went for rent. I attended Catholic school where we wore uniforms, so fortunately I didn't need many clothes.

I was angry. How could my parents take a fantastic and thrilling holiday while I was left with Mrs. Ada? To get back at them, I had my hair cut in a modish style about an inch long. I got a lot of satisfaction out of that because I knew how much it would upset them, especially my mother. I didn't care, though. Mrs. Ada was awful. When I was sick a couple of times, she said she was afraid of catching "a childhood illness," so I stayed in my room and she left meager trays of terrible food outside my door. She also had a bad habit of reading my mail.

Years later, I saw what I thought was Mrs. Ada's ghost at a bank in London not long after my father died. But truly, it was Mrs. Ada, in flesh and blood, and she recognized me. She was one hundred and two, and she invited my husband, Robert, and me to tea. We sat primly in her tiny rickety chairs, and I prayed that Robert's would not collapse.

At the boarding house, Mrs. Ada's practice was to lock her tenants out of the house if we stayed out past midnight. A boyfriend with a Vespa, an Italian scooter like the moped that was all the rage at the time, used to take me to a place called Heaven and Hell, where we could hear great rock 'n' roll. A couple of times, I got back to Mrs. Ada's after midnight and rang the bell, but she would not let me in. I slept on the porch at least twice.

Paulette and Tony came to London for three weeks around Christmas that year. They ignored my complaints about Mrs. Ada. Aunt Alice and Richard, then living in Cyprus, were also in London for a visit. My parents were having a wonderful time, and nothing was going to dampen their enjoyment.

As I had hoped, my mother was horrified by my modish one-inch long haircut. However, my father kept whispering to her, "Just ignore it." There were other tensions, as well, besides my shocking coiffure. We agreed that I would never again just leave an airplane in mid-journey without telling anyone. A small concession since I had already made my point.

Back in Hong Kong, I had been close to completing high school. To attend university, I was required to pass two "A" level exams, but I had taken only one because my parents had made it clear that, while they were paying for Jean-Pierre to go to college, I would not be going. An important reason was financial, but they also said I needed to find a husband, not go to university. I was angry, but I also thought, "This is the way things are and there's nothing you can do about it."

Jean-Pierre was in the last year of his university studies during the time I was at staying at Mrs. Ada's. He was living with Edith, a close friend of my mother's who had recently been widowed. I did not realize it at the time, but Edith and Jean-Pierre were having an affair that lasted several years. It was another of those things no one talked about, although my mother must have been aware of what was going on because she no longer mentioned Edith and had stopped communicating with her.

It was a long time after Jean-Pierre and Edith's relationship ended before my mother reestablished the friendship that began during their kindergarten years. No one ever asked why a twenty-year-old young man would be attracted to a fifty-year-old woman, why Jean-Pierre would be drawn to his mother's friend, or how much all this had to do with rebellion rather than love, or even sexual attraction.

I was never invited to Edith's house when Jean-Pierre was living there, but he and I would sometimes meet at a restaurant for a meal. I was studying a lot to prepare for my "A" level exams, but I was also lonely and homesick. Jean-Pierre was working a part-time job at a nightclub in Soho. I did not know what he did there but he claimed to be a bouncer, which surprised me, because Jean-Pierre stands at five-feet-seven-inches tall and is of a particularly slight build. Nevertheless, he would tell me outlandish tales of fights he had broken up and of gangsters he had single-handedly removed from the premises. He always looked nervous and tense, and his old habit of rubbing the palms of his hands together repeatedly until they must have become calloused had intensified.

"If I don't call you or show up for a while, don't worry," he would tell me. "Important people want retribution. They want to do away with me."

His stories were so improbable, I never knew what to make of them, or what to say. I asked him if he was scared.

"I don't have emotions and, if I did, I would not let them get in my way," he told me.

When we talked, it was only about his escapades. If I changed the subject, he would cut me short. We never confided in each other. I was mad at my parents for leaving me in London at a boarding house for an entire school year while they went on a cruise around the world. I was pretty sure that he resented my parents' move to Hong Kong, but he would never admit it. Although London had become our temporary base, and Hong Kong my parents' temporary home, neither Jean-Pierre nor I had known a real home since our departure from Cairo. We had British passports, but we did not think of ourselves as British. Everywhere I went, I felt like a squatter who at any minute could be evicted. It would not surprise me if Jean-Pierre had suffered similar sentiments. But we never talked about our homeless state, or for that matter anything of substance, anything even verging on the intimate.

I went back to Hong Kong that summer and Jean-Pierre got a job as a geologist in Bamako, the capital of Mali. We did not know it at the time, but we were both soon to embark on nomadic lives— lives filled with travel and change but devoid of stability. It was our fate but it also was the destiny of many of the people we had grown up with in Cairo, people with passports but no country.

Jean-Pierre and I said our farewells one evening in July on Kensington High Street after a quick meal at a dark, gloomy Italian restaurant. We sat in a booth and ate spaghetti with a heavy Bolognese sauce, the kind I disliked and that reminded me of meals at my paternal grandmother's house in Cairo. Jean-Pierre was chain smoking. He kept a cigarette lit all through dinner. I had taken up smoking, so he gave me a couple of cigarettes, the unfiltered French kind that made me cough.

I wanted to say something momentous, something that mattered, but the words did not come. We left the restaurant and stood on the street for a minute. Though it was after 9 p.m., the sky was still bright and clear. (The sun sets late in London in the summer.) My boarding house was to the left; the tube that would take him home was to the right. I gave him a hug. I felt hollow and alone.

"I will miss you," I told him.

"Bye," he said unceremoniously, and turned around and walked away.

I did not see him again for twelve years.

He spent three years in Mali, a year or two in Gabon, and then two or three years in Zaire. He worked in gold and copper mines. I asked him once why he was drawn to geology and he gave me one of his typically cynical, unsatisfactory answers implying his lack of love or attachment to anything.

"I am no good at physics. Geology is the only science degree you can get where you don't need physics," he said.

Michele and her cousin Daniele in Cairo at about two years old. They were born seven days apart. Daniele still bears the scar where Michele hit her with a toy shovel when they were both four.

Michele's paternal grandmother who was always remembered as a "smiley" lady.

Michele's parents, Tony and Paulette, honeymooning at the beach in 1936.

PARŒCIA S. JOSEPH

SPONSI B. V. MARIÆ

TESTIMONIUM MATRIMONII
IN DEI NOMINE: AMEN.

Omnibus et singulis, ad quos pertinet, Ego infrascriptus Parochus hujus Ecclesiæ S. Joseph Sponsi B.V. Mariæ, fidem facio ac testor, quod : prout invenitur in libro Matrimoniorum *IV* Pag *48* Num *53*

Antonius Trigaci

filius *Josephi Trigaci* et *Stellae Lerioti* natione *Melitensis* natus *in Zeitoun* die *7* mensis *Martii* anni *1911* baptizatus in Parœcia *B.M.V. Zeitoun* die —— mensis —— anni *1911* legitimum contraxit Matrimonium in hac Parœcia die *27* mensis *Augusti* anni *1936* cum

Pauletta Harari

filia *Nathan Harari* et *Camillae Amiel* natione *Aegyptia* nata *Cairi* die *29* mensis *Aprilis* anni *1913*. ptizata in Parœcia —— die —— mensis —— anni ——

Testes fuere : *Vincentius Trigaci* et *Richardus Trigaci.*

In quorum fidem, etc.

Datum ex officio Parochiali Sancti Joseph Sponsi B. V. Mariæ, Cairi Ægypti

die *27* mensis *Augusti* anni 1936.

Vice Parochus

P. Eugen Stanett

TAXA P. T *10.* -

Tony and Paulette's wedding certificate issued on 27th of August, 1936, all in Latin in Cairo, Egypt.

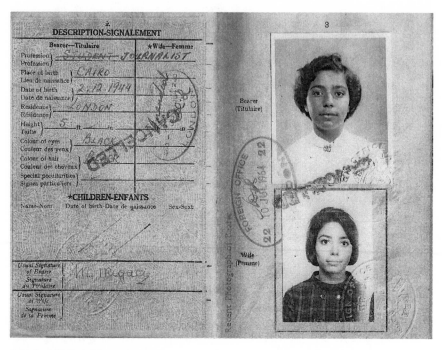

Michele's British passport

Michele in London soon after the family's exile.

Michele at 16—a professional photographer's portrait.

In Hong Kong, Michele dines with her parents.

Michele posing near a scenic spot in
Hong Kong, age 16.

Tony playing bridge in Hong Kong, one of his favorite pastimes. He became well known for his skill.

Tony and Michele enjoy a party together at the Hong Kong Jockey Club.

Congressman Lamar Smith with Michele and the judge at her citizenship ceremony in San Antonio, Texas, in 1997.

Michele and Robert at their wedding in Austin, January 9, 1999.

Michele and her cousin Denyse at Michele's wedding. Denyse had hosted Michele's first wedding three decades before.

Michele with one of her favorite aunts, Alice, in 2000.

Michele at St. Edward's University shaking hands with President George Martin, when she received her Bachelor of Liberal Studies at age 58—a dream realized.

Michele in her kitchen on Cat Mountain treating her journalism students to some of her fine cooking.

Professor Tim Green and Michele enjoy a quiet laugh on the campus of St. Edward's University.

Michele in full teaching mode in the journalism classroom she so enjoyed.

Michele shows off her new "hairstyle" and signature smile, even after her first brain surgery.

13

Working in Hong Kong and Marriage
1962 - 1965

*I*nstead of going to college after I graduated from high school in 1962, I went to work for the first time on a newspaper, the *Hong Kong Standard*. I was assigned to the women's section, and I wrote about weddings. The trouble was that I did not know the difference between one wedding gown fabric and another. I loathed my assignment. One of my mother's friends, who had helped me get the position, suggested I offer to do a different job at the newspaper for three months without pay. I was only seventeen, and I was terrified to approach my bosses. However, I wanted to cover meatier subjects, so I followed the advice and was assigned cops and courts. There were certainly pros and cons to this assignment. On the one hand, it was better than covering weddings. But on the other hand, I had no training at all, and now, no pay. Nevertheless, I was the only woman in Hong Kong covering real news.

The staff was made up of Australians, who frequently made sport of me. A keg of beer arrived regularly in the newsroom at 6 p.m., and one night they said, "We're going to have to teach you to drink." I worked twelve hours a day, and I had to try to be one of them. So I drank. I would have two beers and be knocked out.

I loved seeing my name in print, but my parents hated it. I had one of the worst fights of my life with my parents about working for a newspaper. My father thought it was a vulgar profession. My mother thought I was never going to find a husband.

But actually, it was in the newsroom of the *Hong Kong Standard* that I met my first husband, Keith Kay. His father, Alfred Kay, an American who worked for Pan American Airways, was our neighbor. Alfred's other son, Kent, had been in school with me, but Keith was two years older and had been attending college in northern California, where his mother lived. On a visit to Hong Kong to try his hand at photography, Keith had suddenly decided to move in with his father.

On September 1, 1962, I was in the newsroom when Hong Kong was struck by one of the worst typhoons in the city's history. A new photographer assigned to cover the story with me walked up and said, "Are you Michele?" I said, "Are you Keith?" We became instant friends, and before long, we grew very close. The day I met him, I fell in love with him. I did not date anybody else again.

We ate in cheap restaurants. We worked nonstop. My parents did not suspect anything was going on between us. However, Keith's father, a former journalist who was fond of me and who had inspired my interest in newspapers, was not pleased.

"Keith is not a person you should become attached to," he warned me.

I asked him, "Why not?"

He said Keith was not a marriageable person, and that he didn't really respect his son. I said, "I think he's terrific. I think he's absolutely wonderful."

For the first ten years of marriage to Keith, I tried to forget Alfred's warning. I did not want to believe he was right. I was so absolutely smitten. We stayed together for twenty-five years, despite some wrenching times. We were happy, on and off, for most of those years, but during the last three or four years we both were miserable. During our marriage, we grew up together and came into our own. We lived and worked in Vietnam during the war. We made a home in some of the world's greatest cities—New York, San Francisco, Hong Kong and Paris. And we had two beautiful children together.

Soon after we met, Keith took a new job as a soundman with CBS, but in no time he was promoted to cameraman. I was equally anxious to advance in my career. I was eighteen and had my eye on the bigger paper, the *South China Morning Post*. It had a vast circulation of three hundred thousand to four hundred thousand, and it covered southern China, the Philippines and all of Southeast Asia. More prestigious than the *Hong Kong Standard*, it also paid three times as much as I was earning. I took a job as a general assignments reporter but soon was covering courts.

There were no 6 p.m. beer keg deliveries at the British-staffed *SCMP*. Everyone was "Mister This" or "Mister That." I was "Miss Trigaci" during the ten or eleven months of my tenure. I was starting to get the hang of being a reporter. I no longer dissolved into tears when my work was criticized, as I had at the *Standard* when an editor had asked, "Is this story written in a language any of us speaks?"

By now, Keith and I had begun to spend a lot of time apart. CBS had assigned him to cover the Vietnam War, and he wanted to spend all of his time there. Neither of us could endure the long separations, so on Christmas Eve 1964 Keith asked me to marry him. Of course, I said yes. I was all of twenty.

Slightly more than a month later, on January 27, 1965, the editor of the *SCMP* came to me one night and said, "Something very strange has just happened. You have been drafted into the American army."

Being a British citizen, not to mention a woman, I took a few minutes to figure out what was happening. Keith was using my office address as his own, and a draft notice for him, addressed to me, had been passed on to the editor. I was horrified. It was one thing for Keith to cover the Vietnam War; it was quite another for him to be fighting in it. I learned we would have to go stateside for Keith's active duty. We went first to Louisiana, then on to New York, and later to New Jersey, where he would be based for eighteen months.

I would be displaced to yet another country, but this time as an adult.

In 1965, as Keith and I prepared to set out for the United States, I was unable to get a visa. The U. S. government could not comprehend my unusual British passport, or my unusual British citizenship, both acquired in the oddest ways.

My father, who had procured my passport during those last days in Cairo, had warned me about all of this. He thought going to America was a terrible idea and that I would run into problems with my passport. I could not really understand why. I went to the immigration office for help and came away afraid I might be deported instead. They finally suggested I try getting citizenship in Canada. I left the office without a visa and without knowing what to do next.

It was as if this passport, once my salvation, was now a barrier to opening the next chapter of my life.

On July 10, 1965, still without a visa officially allowing me to be in the U.S., I married Keith at my cousin Denyse Milton's spacious apartment in Manhattan. My mother traveled to the wedding, but my father did not—partly because he didn't think the marriage would last and partly for financial reasons. My parents worried about the kind of life I would have, being married to a journalist who was enthralled by Vietnam and who thought nothing of having me hitchhike around the world with him.

However, in time they both grew to love Keith, just as my mother's family had learned to love Tony. In fact, throughout 1990, the year Keith and I divorced, I did not visit my parents because I knew it would not be a pleasant reunion. These same parents who had been dead set against my marriage were now dead set against my divorce.

14

New York - Saigon - Hong Kong - San Francisco
1965 - 1968

*D*uring Keith's stint in the army, we lived in New York. I loved the city, but once again I was a stranger in a strange land and felt unwelcome. Alone on the streets, I was doubly stressed trying to navigate both the city and the culture. Once I got lost trying to find my way to Flushing, Queens. I could not even find the entrance to the subway. Timidly, trying to mask the desperation in my voice, I asked a man on the street, "Do you know where the tube is?" He backed away, very slowly. The tube? Surely, I was a kook.

My worst subway experience, however, occurred during my first summer in the city. I was riding a crowded train, standing in high-heeled shoes, tired and anxious to get home. All of a sudden, the train lurched to an abrupt stop and everything went black. It was the great New York City blackout of November 1965. I stood in the dark for what seemed like an eternity. Finally, when my feet could no longer take it and I thought I might pass out from the heat, I asked some of my fellow sufferers if we might take turns sitting, and maybe rotate every fifteen or thirty minutes. The seated people would not hear of it.

Many of the trapped passengers were smoking, so the overheated train car smelled terrible. Unfortunately, the only way I was able to rest my aching feet for a few minutes was by giving a teenager a cigarette in exchange for a seat. I wondered what I had gotten myself into by coming to New York. By the time I arrived home later that night, Keith was fast asleep, not the least bit worried about me. I wasn't terribly surprised. He was self-absorbed and already cheating on me. I had come to understand what Alfred had meant when he had warned me about his son, but while from time to time I flirted with the idea of leaving him, I did not pursue it. Despite his flaws, I loved my husband and found life with him irresistibly interesting.

Meanwhile, Keith persisted in asking his army superiors to ship him to Vietnam. He told them he could be of some use as an army photographer, but his commanding officer told him to forget it. He would be staying at the base in New Jersey. While Keith dreamed of Vietnam, I lived without a resident visa in mortal fear of being deported. Keith's military outfit knew of my predicament and eventually helped me acquire a temporary visa. With that in hand, I found a job with the Pakistan mission to the U.N. Then I went to work for about six months at Pfizer, promoting new drugs. Finally, I landed a job that brought me closer to my real love— newspapers—writing for a pharmaceutical trade magazine. This was the best I could do at the time. I had tried to get an interview at *The New York Times* but could not even get a toe in the door.

The day Keith was mustered out of the army, we packed up and left for Vietnam. We were young and broke. We had only enough money to buy one-way tickets. My father gave us a couple of hundred bucks. Illogically, we decided to stay in the very best hotel in Saigon because Keith thought that would impress a prospective employer. One week ticked by, two weeks passed, then three weeks. We were just about out of money and practically desperate. During the fourth week, CBS finally hired Keith back as a cameraman. Keith's father, Alfred, hired me to work for him at Pan American in Saigon. My job was to take care of the GIs flying out of Vietnam for rest and recuperation. I was the troubleshooter. There were three flights a day, and they kept me pretty busy. If a soldier on a flight was having a birthday, I procured a cake for the flight. If something went wrong with a flight, I was the person who listened to the screaming, and I was expected to make things right. We also took photos of everybody getting onto the planes, and later I mailed the pictures to the soldiers' families back in the States. Somehow, I also found time to write freelance pieces for *Asia* magazine.

We stayed in Vietnam for two years, and Keith won an Emmy for his work there. When I found out I was pregnant, my first thought was that Vietnam was no place to have a baby. The hospitals in Saigon had three or four people to a room, and overall they were quite uncomfortable places. We decided that the baby should be born in Hong Kong, where my parents lived. I could stay with them for a few weeks—that is, if I could get there at all. The planes out of Saigon accommodated only a few people at once, and I could never be certain I would be able to board one of them when the time came. Unbeknownst to me, when I decided to try to leave, my parents had begun taking turns camping out at the airport in Hong Kong for a week, waiting for me, not knowing which flight, or even which day, I would arrive. The day I finally landed, there was Tony, waiting patiently for me. My parents took me home with them, and Keith followed two days later.

Our daughter was born on June 23, 1968, in a nursing facility. We agreed she was stunning, and she immediately dazzled Keith. Still, I was twenty-three and terrified. My life seemed to be speeding up, everything was happening too fast. Keith said CBS was sending him to San Francisco. He would leave soon, and I would stay behind for a while with my parents. My daughter was six weeks old when I would again uproot myself to become a stranger once more, this time with a new baby.

In San Francisco in the late 1960s, Keith shot footage for stories about hippies and protesters. I had a part-time job in public relations. I liked the city, its vibrancy and variety. However, Keith traveled a lot, and I did not like being alone so much. He took any assignment that would take him out of town, always hoping for something more exciting than the last.

Once again, I found myself in a place that was completely foreign. I was always saying or doing the wrong thing. I was lonely and I wanted to belong, but the effort required to fit in made me tired and even lonelier. Once I asked a neighbor who was in the Junior League if I could join. She looked horrified. I did not know that it was the kind of organization you are *asked* to join, not one you can ask to join.

15

Hong Kong, Paris and Dallas

1969-1984

*I*n 1969, after a bad year in San Francisco, I told Keith, "I'm going back to Hong Kong." I had never learned to feel at home in San Francisco. I missed my friends and family. I had no support system. Keith did not argue. We went back to Hong Kong, where we rented an apartment. He traveled back and forth to Saigon to report once again on events in Vietnam, and I went back to work for the *South China Morning Post*.

Life settled down a bit, and our son was born in 1972.

My bosses decided they wanted me to start a health-oriented magazine, the *Asian Journal of Medicine*. Eventually, it circulated all over Southeast Asia, and I made a good salary.

In 1972, Karen McDonald and I wrote *The Hong Kong Shopper*, which I updated and expanded in 1976. Also in 1976, I wrote *Doing Business in Hong Kong* for the American Chamber of Commerce in Hong Kong. All three books sold well. Unbelievably, they are still available on Amazon.com. I also freelanced for the *South China Morning Post.* I worked for the magazine *Asian Journal of Medicine* forty hours a week and freelanced at night. I did not sleep much, but fortunately, I did not seem to need to in those days.

The Vietnam War began to wind down as we were moving back to Hong Kong. The peace talks had started in 1968, and by the time we arrived in Hong Kong, they had just about figured out the table shapes. The Paris Accords of 1973 required all external troops to be withdrawn, but another two years would elapse before the war officially ended. However, Keith did not want it to be over. He stayed in Vietnam as long as he could. He was aboard one of the last helicopters out of Saigon in 1975, from the Pittman apartment complex, the same CIA facility that everyone has seen as the "last helicopter leaving" so often in the news. He arrived in Hong Kong on a boat, and promptly went to bed with a couple of cases of whiskey.

Keith could not cope with a young family and all the resulting responsibilities. He was out of the war. He had lost his purpose; he had lost his people. He was so depressed; I thought he had gone crazy.

Somehow, though, he managed to keep his job with CBS, and slowly pulled himself together. CBS asked him whether he would like to go next to Paris or to Israel. I had been to Israel several times and loved it. Of all the places I had been since our family's exile from Egypt, Israel felt most like home. I chose Israel, but we went to Paris, where I spent the first three months looking for a place for us to live. When I finally found an apartment, it had no sink or appliances. These "conveniences" had to be purchased separately. In 1976, we moved to the seventh arrondissement on the Left Bank, not far from Napoleon's grave and very near the tourist areas and well-to-do neighborhoods. We lived there for five years, but we also lived for several months in Tel Aviv, so I got part of my wish.

Before living in Paris, I spoke French only to my mother. Afterwards I could speak French with all of France. To this day, Jean-Pierre and I still converse almost exclusively in French.

In Paris, I took a job with the U.S. Chamber of Commerce, which promoted American jobs in Hong Kong. I started a magazine for them, a glossy monthly. Although I had the title of editor, I also wrote articles. I had a freelance staff, and we covered business news. It was fun, but with two young children and a husband who traveled all the time, I had a lot to juggle. Luckily, I had a live-in nanny, Laura, who spoiled me. She brought me coffee in bed and cleaned for us.

Keith was not prospering the way I was, unfortunately. He was having problems at work, and his bosses at CBS were growing impatient with him. Keith was petulant. If he did not like an assignment, he would refuse to do it. Perhaps because he had been successful so young, he had developed the mistaken idea that he could run the show wherever he went. CBS retaliated. The bosses sent him to Dallas, as bureau chief.

Back in the States once again, I was reminded daily that this was not my country. With their American father, my children were U.S. citizens, but I had never taken the steps to become one. Consequently, I was not allowed even to stand in the same immigration line with my children. No one would explain why I had to leave them standing apart from me, so I grew frustrated and angry. I have often noticed how the immigration officials are not so nice to people who are not American.

The children and I were to meet Keith at the Anatole Hotel in Dallas. When we arrived, we found a note from him saying he was gone on assignment and that the room had not yet been paid for, although CBS had said it would be paying for two rooms. The Anatole refused us a room until I threw a complete hissy fit.

Eventually, we moved to Rockwall, a Dallas suburb, in 1981. Keith was required to maintain budgets as bureau chief. He had no interest in accounting, so I managed all of his budgets for him.

I found a job as editor of the *Dallas/Fort Worth Business Journal,* but, fresh from Paris and other foreign parts, I did not know much about U.S. dollars, and I knew even less about the Securities and Exchange Commission. I came home and cried every day. Ignorance, isolation and loneliness were once again my lot and daily companions. Eventually I overcame my unhappiness and grew to like the work, but it turned out that moving to Rockwall had been a bad decision.

The kids had to be alone for several hours at the house after school. I couldn't dash home and back to work to be with them. Once I got home from work, I could not bear to go back out into the maze of strip malls and cookie-cutter suburbs that were nearly impossible to navigate. I was afraid I could not find my way home again. Keith was always gone. He claimed to be playing tennis, and CBS was constantly angry with him for one thing or another.

Finally, his bosses told him he would do better financially if he worked on contract. He became a freelancer. But as time went by, he grew more and more unreasonable and disagreeable. He refused to file his tax documents. We got into trouble with the IRS because he refused to report his earnings accurately. The IRS investigated him while I looked on in horror.

16

Texas & Washington, D.C.; a New Passport

1984-2008

*I*n 1984, after working for a few years for the *Dallas/Fort Worth Business Journal*, I took a job as editor of *Texas Business Magazine*, a job that involved considerable travel. Keith and I took turns staying with the kids. I had an apartment and a car in Houston, as well as a car in Dallas. The job and the money were great. Keith was still freelancing for CBS. He covered the war in Iran. I worked for the magazine until it suddenly went out of business. In retrospect, I can see what happened. It was the only company I have ever worked for that did not require employees to document their expense accounts. If you said, "I need two thousand dollars," they gave you two thousand dollars, no questions asked.

The magazine closed abruptly one Friday in 1988. I had had no warning. I was absolutely stunned to find myself unemployed through no fault of my own. I called a friend, Angelous Angelou, and asked him if he knew of any job openings. He said the *Austin American-Statesman* was looking for a business editor. "It is the job for you," he said. "Call George Sutton, the ME."

I called Sutton, the managing editor, first thing Monday morning. He said, "We need someone quickly."

My son was already in Austin attending St. Stephen's Episcopal School for his sophomore year. I had sent him there because I was not thrilled with the excessive emphasis on sports in Dallas area schools. I really wanted to be in Austin as well, and I desperately wanted that job. My daughter was already married and had a baby, so she would stay in Dallas.

I arrived in Austin early in the morning for the *Statesman* interview and borrowed a car from a friend. I told her I would need it for only "an hour or two." I didn't get finished with my interviews until 7 p.m. When I returned the car, my friend was mad, but it was worth it. I got the job that day.

I had no qualms about leaving Rockwall, although I would miss being close to my daughter and her family. Apart from that, I had never fitted in there, never felt at home, and had not met many interesting people. I had never found my niche. I had played a lot of tennis, but I hadn't had many deep conversations. But, whereas I had felt disconnected from the people in Rockwall, I did not feel that way in Austin. With its big university, the city attracted people from all over world—people like me.

I decided to move to Austin and find an apartment. Initially, I would stay with my friend Sally. I decided Keith could fend for himself. I wasn't going to help him with the rent. I didn't love him anymore, and I certainly didn't trust him. His affairs used to drive me nuts, but I had finally grown used to his disloyalty and no longer cared.

Keith, however, followed me to Austin. In the middle of my move, I had to go to London because my father was having heart problems. After I came back Keith found a house in Wimberley. I spent most nights there and some at Sally's apartment. She was never at home because she was in the process of moving to Dallas, so I eventually kept her apartment. Once, when I drove to Wimberley, Keith had another woman's belongings and her photos all over the house. I was so angry I took all of my clothes, put them in the back seat of my car and drove back to Austin. I decided on that day to leave Keith. But it would take me two years to complete the divorce. First, I waited for my son to graduate from high school, and then, in July 1990, I went to the courthouse. Jim Phillips, my longtime friend from the *Statesman*, was there waiting for me. He lent me a strong shoulder to lean on throughout the ordeal.

He and other members of the *Statesman* staff were like family to me. On the business desk, I worked with Kim Tyson, Kirk Ladendorf, Michelle Breyer, Lori Hawkins, Kyle Pope, and Earl Golz, and for a while we had Chuck Lindell as a copyeditor, along with Tony Shuga. We went to lunch every day and were a close-knit bunch. On the day of our divorce, Keith was in the Middle East working on a story, my parents were in England, my brother was in Spain, my daughter was in Dallas, and my son was only eighteen. I felt alone again, and sad.

My divorce from Keith was decreed in two minutes. Nothing was disputed.

I held a number of different jobs at the *Statesman*. Around 1991, I became an editorial writer. I liked writing editorials and I wrote a column every Sunday, but I couldn't get along with the editorial page editor at the time. Sometimes I would become so angry that I would get up and walk out of his office. When the Washington, D. C., bureau job opened up in 1993, I went after it.

This was also the year I quit smoking. It was another bad year.

The Washington job was a fascinating one, but for a variety of reasons I was unhappy working in the Cox bureau. In Washington, D.C., the fact that I was not a U. S. citizen hit me hard. Here I was at the seat of government, a government I didn't fully understand, and I was slowly beginning to realize I had more and more of a stake in the laws that were being made there. One day I was sitting in Texas Congressman Lamar Smith's office when he said he was supporting a bill that would make it harder for people who were not Americans to become citizens.

"Congressman, please don't do that," I said.

I proceeded to tell him I was not a citizen. And when I told Lamar that when I first came to America, I was an illegal immigrant, he nearly had a heart attack.

"Does your employer know that?" he asked.

"They never asked," I said, "and I never told them."

The idea of becoming a U.S. citizen had been running through my mind for some time. After divorcing my American husband, I had thought of going back to Europe, but such a move wouldn't have made sense. My job was in the States. My children are Americans. Although my British citizenship had been conferred by an act of Parliament at the request of the Queen herself, I didn't feel as though I truly had a country. America might as well become my country, and if it was to be my country, I should become a U.S. citizen.

Becoming a citizen would not only give me a sense of belonging, it would also help solve some practical problems. As a non-citizen, I couldn't buy a house, and traveling was difficult. I had a British passport, but not a U.S. passport. So anytime I traveled I had to have a visa. The kids had different visas, and all of this was a nuisance.

One stumbling block was that I didn't want to give up my British citizenship. I told Lamar all of this, and he said, "Whatever day you decide to become an American, I will fly to San Antonio and be your sponsor." He was true to his word, but the event wouldn't take place until some time after that conversation. Lamar also introduced legislation to allow dual citizenship

I returned to Austin from Washington, D.C., in June 1995 after Rich Oppel became the *Statesman* editor. I took a job on the state desk covering the legislature.

By March 1997, I was ready to become a citizen. I had filled out all of the paperwork and taken the test. Most of the test questions were quite elementary. A few of them stymied everyone in the newsroom. I passed the test and dropped a note to Lamar telling him to prepare to come to San Antonio for the official swearing-in ceremony.

At the citizenship ceremony in San Antonio, Lamar Smith was there, as promised, along with my son. Tears welled in my eyes as I thought about what it meant to become part of a country so vast and so diverse. People from all over the world were at that ceremony, and they all were taking the oath that day to be loyal to America. I was so nervous, I couldn't even remember the words to the Pledge of Allegiance, but it didn't matter. I became an American.

I never got around to telling my father that I had become an American, but I think he would have been pleased. He died two months after my citizenship was official. I had wanted to tell him in person.

I went to England for his funeral without having yet obtained a U. S. passport. Getting out of the country was easy. Getting back in was a big problem because my being a U.S. citizen produced a complication. Unlike in previous years, the immigration authorities in Chicago now didn't want to let me in with a British passport because I was an American. They put me in a tiny room while they conferred over my status. I was there so long I began sobbing. Finally, one of the American officers came in and I tried to explain my situation, and why I had delayed getting a U. S. passport. He firmly said I should plan no more travel without this essential document. I came home and the next day mailed a check to Houston to get the passport. They fined me $500, which was a lot of money to me in those days, and then it took them a year to clear the check.

In such odd ways at different times throughout my life, a simple little black book called a passport has often threatened to alter the course of my destiny.

Predictably, my mother and Jean-Pierre were not pleased about my newly minted citizenship and did not understand why I wanted it. I still felt I had done the right thing. The U. S. and Texas started feeling more like home, and I began to settle back into the rhythms of Austin.

By mid-1997 I had been single for seven years. Soon after my father died, and in the midst of my grief, I realized how much I needed a partner, a friend and someone to love. One of the best strokes of luck in my entire life came when a neighbor introduced me to Robert Schultz who, like me, was recently divorced and very lonely. We were drawn to one another immediately. Though I wasn't immediately sure that another marriage was what I wanted, I thought he was wonderful then, and I still do.

We dated for a year and a half, and we married on January 9, 1999, at St. David's Episcopal Church in downtown Austin. The wedding was followed by a luncheon in a ballroom at the Four Seasons Hotel, with its windows that look out across the Colorado River. My mother and my cousin Denyse from Ft. Lauderdale came, and so did my children. Jean-Pierre, of course, wasn't there. He visited the United States only once, when I still lived in Dallas.

I had spent part of the year prior to my second marriage working as press secretary for John Cornyn, who had left the Texas Supreme Court to run against Democrat Jim Mattox for attorney general in 1998. After he beat Mattox, I moved on to policy work for Carole Keeton Strayhorn in the state comptroller's office. I liked her very much, but she was demanding to work for, to say the least. She would call me from somewhere out of town and say she needed some information—for instance, statistics on how many children went to school in three or four different places over the last ten years—and she needed it right now. I'd object that I couldn't find all of that information so quickly, but I'd start scrambling to get it. Ten minutes later, she'd call back wanting something more. I stayed in that position for two or three months, took a break for a month-long trip to China with Robert, and decided that I was not right for the job.

After that, I did some private consulting, and I made more money than ever before. I rented office space from George Christian, and I wrote Neal Spelce's political newsletter. I worked with Maggie Balough, the former editor of the *Statesman*. None of this work was difficult or as stressful as being a politician's press secretary, so I enjoyed all of it, and usually went home around three o'clock.

Still, something was missing in my life, and I was never going to feel complete without it. I wanted a college education. There were essential facts of American life I knew nothing about, particularly American history and government. I didn't fully understand how the state and federal governments were set up. Years before, when I was working at the *Statesman*, with minimum advance notice, I was sent to Houston on a 6:30 a.m. flight to cover news of a judicial ruling on redistricting. I got on the plane but had no idea what "redistricting" was. The political writer for the *Dallas Morning News*, Sam Attlesey, explained it all to me on the plane ride. He was a gem, but I became intensely aware that I no longer wanted to have to ask these kinds of questions of other people all the time. Such gaps in my education made me feel like a stranger in my adopted country.

When I told friends and family that I wanted to get a bachelor's degree, some of them thought I was crazy. Why would I want to go to college in my fifties? My mother thought the idea was ridiculous. Only Robert supported me. He said no matter how much it cost, he would pay for it. Happily, I enrolled in New College at St. Edward's University, which is a program for adult students with work experience that can be evaluated to count for college credits. While I went to college, I continued to write a column on Sundays for the paper. I was ecstatic to be able to pursue my life's goal and still write for a newspaper. Since it was a column and not breaking news, I could write it on any day of the week when I found the time.

I loved school. I was able to take classes in subjects I didn't know anything about. I found the coursework easy enough, except for math, but Robert, an engineer, turned the dining room into a math tutoring room so that he could help me. Forever patient, he helped me work every problem in a set, even if only every other problem was assigned. He helped me complete every extra-credit assignment even after I maxed out the available extra points. I completed my undergraduate degree in December 2002. This gave me a sense of personal accomplishment, and I felt more connected to America, and to Texas, than ever before. But I still yearned to learn more. I set my sights on getting a master's degree, and perhaps a doctorate.

But first I needed to think about acquiring some good health insurance for myself and for Robert, who had retired. I found out that if I returned to work at the *Statesman* for several more months, I would be eligible for retiree health benefits, so I went back in January 2003. The next seven months became a trial of my patience. The legislature was in session, and I was assigned to write about topics such as the controversy over automatic admission of the top ten percent of Texas high school graduates to the University of Texas and the other state universities. This topic, along with several others I was asked to cover, didn't interest me. I had been to college, and my ideas about how I wanted to spend my time had changed. I had never been bored before, and that's how I knew I was finished with journalism and ready to return to St. Edward's.

In May 2005, I completed my master's degree in liberal arts. I loved the program. It was exactly what I wanted and required no more math. Parts of this memoir, in an earlier form, were my master's thesis. The idea to write about my lifelong experience of displacement had just come to me one day in a flash.

I had started to wonder how I had come to feel at home in Austin. After all, there are a lot of very different kinds of people in this city. Some of them never travel and think San Antonio is far away, but in Austin there are also people from distant lands, people who speak languages the average American citizen might never even have heard spoken before. I had never heard some of these languages before, either.

I began my thesis with an essay about why my family had left Egypt. The other essays flowed from that one. As I wrote, I learned a lot about myself, about my own as well as my parents' and brother's sense of displacement. I realized how very different I am, even from some of my closest friends, because unlike me, they feel completely at home wherever they are. Some even fly flags to show their allegiance to home. I can't imagine hanging a flag outside my door, not even the flag that flew at the Texas Capitol while I was taking my oath of citizenship, the one that Dave McNeely gave me. State Representative Dianne Delisi gave me another flag when I left the *Statesman*. I appreciated the gifts, but I never flew either flag because I couldn't find a feeling in myself that would have motivated me to do so.

I started to explore, through my writing, this and other features in myself that I had never really thought about before. My parents' stories surprised me when I wrote them down. I didn't realize exactly what I knew, or who they were, until I wrote down their stories. I realized that I would feel uneasy showing the essays to my mother, to Jean-Pierre or even to my cousins in Paris. Some of the pieces that were very personal aroused a variety of emotions in me, some of them uncomfortable. Writing didn't make me cry, but recalling those days awakened memories and feelings I had put aside for years. I began to understand a little better how my brother, Jean-Pierre, had chosen to wall off and deny so many of his memories and emotions.

After I had completed my master's degree, I began teaching a few courses for St. Edward's. I discovered that I enjoyed teaching. I stopped thinking about pursuing a doctorate. When a position opened in journalism in the English Writing Program, some of the faculty felt I was just right for the job. I agreed to work at St. Edward's for three years. My goal was to create a journalism program and to re-create the student newspaper. I loved being an adviser to the school paper. My favorite part was working with the students. I enjoyed teaching my students what a story is, and how to approach writing it. At the beginning, I scared them, but after we got to know one another, I'd have them all over to dinner. I didn't think of myself as a teacher. I was only somebody with a passion for journalism who wanted to share it with them.

Retiring after three years was always part of the plan but, if I had not accomplished my goal, I would have been willing to stay longer. At the end of those three years, in May 2008, I was ready to quit and begin to spend more time with my husband and family. Still, I felt a little melancholy because I loved the work so much. However, I realized I hadn't missed daily journalism. Looking back, I know I always liked reporting, but I really never liked being an editor.

I would have been happy to spend a few more years working in journalism, but I wish I had not spent all that time in Dallas.

Instead, I wish I had been a freelance foreign correspondent in Africa. Except for North Africa, where I was born, I know little about Africa, and it interests me.

In a way, working in Paris was like being a foreign correspondent. For a while I thought about going back to Paris after the kids were grown. But America had so much to offer me that moving to France or England didn't make sense. The children were here, and I had health care here. Over there, I wouldn't have put in enough years for a pension. And the houses are all tiny. Most important of all, I would never have met Robert.

17

Jean-Pierre, an Enigma
1970-2009

*M*y brother's life had been as nomadic as my own, but unlike me, he never married. By 1970, he was living in a mining town in Western Australia. He corresponded with my parents. His letters contained stories tinged with the same tone and bravado as his earlier Soho tales. He wrote about encounters with angry tribes, of harrowing travel through the bush, of corrupt political leaders. The stories would have been fascinating had they not sounded so fabricated and far-fetched and so sorely lacking in normal sentiment and emotion.

I often sent my brother change-of-address cards and birth announcements, but I never received any acknowledgment. Eventually, in 1984, while the children and I were still living in Hong Kong, he wrote to my parents telling them that life in the outback had become too solitary and tedious and that he wanted to come to Hong Kong and look for a job.

I went to the airport to pick him up. I had not seen him since I was a schoolgirl in London, so I was not even sure I would recognize him. But when I saw a slight, balding man standing in the main hall at Kai Tak Airport, looking around anxiously and rubbing the palms of his hands, I knew it was Jean-Pierre. He had changed, but he had not lost that trademark. He had lost a lot of hair, and he looked older, browner, and thinner.

He gave me a perfunctory kiss, looked surprised that my children were with me, patted them on the head, and started walking toward the car park. This was the first time he had met my children. He made no comment at all about the children. He did not remark on how beautiful they were, or how well behaved. It was as though he had seen them many times before.

"Did you have a good trip?" I asked.

"It was very long. I had to change several planes. And in that part of Australia, you never know when planes are going to crash," he answered. Why planes crashed with such frequency there—and without making the news—was not evident or explained.

Jean-Pierre got a job in Hong Kong with a brokerage firm and found an apartment. He spent the next three years in Hong Kong and I saw him often. I would run into him in town; we would occasionally meet for lunch and we would see each other at Paulette and Tony's house on Sundays. I introduced him to my friends and he seemed more social, more outgoing than in earlier years. He even started dating an American woman his age. I got to know him a little better during those years and grew to realize that he was intelligent and remarkably well-read and informed in both economics and politics.

He had acquired a staccato style of speech that underscored his intensity. He spoke fast, in short sentences, with an air of authority that made me hesitate to question his statements or logic. Jean-Pierre did not make small talk or say things he had not thought through. We talked a lot back then about the market, particularly at my parents' house, where investments became the only interest my father and Jean-Pierre had in common.

Being forced out of Egypt had been difficult for all of us, but I began to think it had left the deepest wound on Jean-Pierre. He seemed to fear closeness to others and to steer away from attachments. I wondered if he had been so devastated by our losses in Egypt in 1956 that he would never again risk a commitment. I also wondered if he was afraid of responsibilities, afraid he would not do things right. Perhaps that is why he tried so hard to have a quixotic persona, a dashing eccentric with no obligations to others. His heavy foreign accent, and his tendency to pepper his English speech with French words and expressions, helped accentuate that facade.

He seemed to avoid attachments to things as well as to people. Jean-Pierre did not seem to own very much. He arrived in Hong Kong with just one suitcase. Perhaps when he destroyed all of his belongings in Cairo, he found it too threatening ever to acquire more. He was always well-dressed but he had a small repertoire— one suit, one sports jacket, several pairs of flannel pants, shirts in pastel colors only, and jeans and a bathing suit for weekends. He did not own a car, and as far I know he had never learned to drive. While he lived in Hong Kong, I never once saw his apartment, nor did my parents. I suspected that his surroundings must have been excessively and embarrassingly Spartan. And although his job and living conditions provided little opportunity for bravado, he had not shed his propensity for telling strange stories. I can only suppose that he believed these tales made him more interesting. He would not give me his address or phone number because he still maintained that people were hunting for him.

"What people?" I would ask.

"It's best you don't know," he would answer.

My growing impatience with his behavior crested when my father suffered a heart attack and I could not reach my brother because I did not have his telephone number. Not until the next morning when he was at the office was I able to get hold of him. By then, Tony was out of the woods after a long, bad night. It was the first time I could remember Jean-Pierre being contrite.

"I am sorry. I will give you my number but you must promise never to give it to anyone else," he said. His words scared me because I had the sense he had truly grown to believe his own nonsense.

But he was sweet to Tony and nice to Paulette during the month after Tony's heart attack when he was home recuperating. And when my daughter had an accident, he came to the hospital and sat with me all night. He never talked, but his presence was comforting, and I forgave him his silences, his distance, and his mistrust of the world.

I even forgave his miserly behavior. Jean-Pierre had always been tight with money but over the years when I did not see him, he seemed to have become even stingier. Many of us in Hong Kong had boats, and we would spend weekends sailing around the colony's islands. Everyone invited to a boat party contributed food and drink. Jean-Pierre always came empty-handed. He would come to my children's birthday parties without a gift. At Christmas, when we gathered at my parents' home to exchange presents, he had brought nothing to exchange. When we went to lunch, he always forgot to bring his wallet.

"I'll do it next time," he would say.

You could not joke and say, "Sure," sarcastically. He would be offended and storm off. It was easier to pay the check and say nothing.

Still, I felt that our renewed relationship held a little promise, that he had become less defensive, that he had come into his own.

He seemed to be enjoying a more conventional life, going to work, having relationships with women his age, and carrying on a social life of sorts. However, those good years ended when the Hong Kong stock market collapsed.

Jean-Pierre returned to London and over time, he took assignments once again in Africa. Eventually he bought a flat in Majorca, Spain, where my mother's friend and his one-time mistress, Edith, was living. It was cheap, he said, and he needed a place to go between assignments. He no longer wanted to live for months and years at a time in Africa. Instead, he went there for short periods, usually to replace others who were either ill or on vacation.

I left Hong Kong shortly after Jean-Pierre did, when Keith and I moved to Paris. Jean-Pierre often came to visit. He seemed content. He had dated a French woman, Anik, while he was a student in London, right after Edith ended their affair. Anik told me many years later that she had wanted to marry Jean-Pierre, but he would not make a commitment to her or to anyone else for that matter. She had eventually left Europe and moved to Ottawa, where she married a Canadian. But she and Jean-Pierre had apparently stayed in touch. She came to Paris frequently to see her family, and she and Jean-Pierre started meeting again. If it was not love, it was a pretty intense infatuation.

They would stay with us—sometimes for several weeks at a time. Both of them drank and smoked heavily. Late at night I would hear them drinking and laughing. I had never noticed his drinking before, but they would down a liter of Scotch before the night was over. When I suggested he buy his own Scotch, he told me I had hurt his feelings and he would not visit us any longer. But he came with Anik anyway, though he brought his own Scotch. I never found out whether she was still married at that point. He seemed more human when he was with her, more normal. She was not particularly attractive and she had a giggle that grated on me.

She was short, plump and had a lazy eye that turned inward and gave her a strange look. But she dressed stylishly, her hair was always well cut, and she had that innate ability of French women to make the most of their attributes. Most interesting to me was that when Jean-Pierre would start to tell one of his strange tales, she would laugh and tell him to stop.

"*Ca suffit,* Jean-Pierre," she would tell him. "It is not true and it is not funny."

Anik seemed to be able to put him in his place and he seemed to like that place. He took from her the criticism that he would not hear from anyone else. He would laugh and hug her.

In 1981, I moved back to the United States. This time, it would be thirteen years before Jean-Pierre and I saw each other again—thirteen years with only an annual card. I occasionally wrote him a letter and sent pictures of the children, but he never answered. Paulette had suggested that he at least send my children birthday cards. He responded by mailing us one card a year—a universal card that wished us all happy birthdays, Mother's Day, Father's Day, Easter, Passover, Christmas and every type of New Years, including Rosh Hashanah and the Chinese and Gregorian new years. He would buy a blank card and write our names and all the holidays in by hand.

Those thirteen years were not good for him. He did not have enough work and he had slipped back into his reclusiveness. At my suggestion, we finally met in London in 1994 to deal with our parents' deteriorating health. We both visited my parents every year, but this time we made plans for our visits to coincide. I had aged and so had he. The major difference I saw in him was that he had stopped drinking. I asked him if quitting had been difficult, but he shrugged me off, denying that he had ever had a problem. He was cold and distant.

"I am not in the mood to drink any longer," he said. "I used to be in the mood and now I am not. That is why I don't drink."

He made a similar statement several years later when he stopped smoking, once again denying both his former addiction and whatever difficulty quitting may have entailed.

I had hoped that we would finally develop some emotional connection, but I was disappointed. I had recently divorced and was going through a lot of financial and emotional turmoil. He did not want to hear any of it. I wanted to talk about the past, about our parents and what we would do when one of them died. That subject also was on his verboten list. When Tony insisted on talking about his will, Jean-Pierre told him that he did not want to be its executor. He said that Tony should not count on him to take care of my mother's financial affairs, should something happen to him. Tony looked surprised but he kept his own counsel. My father had learned that when he argued with Jean-Pierre, Paulette would immediately take her son's side and the disagreement would grow into a family row, something he preferred to avoid.

In the end, we talked about the weather, we commiserated about how gloomy London felt in the winter, and we engaged in other occasional small talk. My parents had a guest room that Jean-Pierre moved into, leaving me the living room couch. I asked if we could switch sleeping quarters halfway through the week. But he told me that he was suffering from intense headaches that often immobilized him for days at a time, and he needed his comfort and privacy. He had started to walk very slowly. This was very odd. We would walk down the hill from my parents' flat to the High Street, ten minutes away, to catch the tube to town, but the walk now took as long as half an hour.

"Jean-Pierre, why are you walking so slowly?" I inquired.

"I always have," he told me.

"No, you haven't."

"Well, it hurts my head to walk fast."

"Have you seen a doctor?"

"No, I don't want to see a doctor."

"You really should."

No answer.

We did not correspond, talk on the phone, or see each other again until three years later, in 1997, when Tony suffered a fatal heart attack. I flew to London from Austin, while Jean-Pierre traveled from Kinshasa in Zaire. Within an hour of my being in London, he told me he would come to the funeral but not to count on him for anything else.

My brother still walked slowly and insisted on taking over the guest room, once again proclaiming his headaches. During the day, he sat on a chair in the living room, crying for hours, his body shivering and shaking. His way of dealing with his pain was to withdraw. He sat at the back of the room at the funeral and stood alone at the reception, avoiding others. I was equally distraught, but my way of coping was to organize the burial and later the reception for my parents' friends, and to make plans to handle my mother's affairs. Jean-Pierre appeared to be in a trance, in a faraway world.

On the night after the funeral, as on that awful day in Cairo more than forty years earlier, Jean-Pierre exploded. He unleashed the anger that must have been brewing for days—and perhaps for decades. It was ugly, violent and unexpected. I had made the mistake of asking him if he thought the funeral was what Tony would have wanted.

"I don't know. I don't care what he wanted. He is gone," he replied. "I just know that I hated it. Your mother hated it. It was so typical of you. So efficient. So cold. Did you do it for us, for him or for you? Everything worked so smoothly; there was no heart to it."

He paused, rubbing his palms and sweating profusely.

"You have nothing but ice in your veins," he shouted at me. "It has always been that way. You are the one who gets things done as though there was some sort of virtue to getting things done. Your father has been lying in his casket all week and you have been running around shuffling papers. You care nothing for your family, for any of us."

This harangue went on for a while—a long while. I was sobbing and shaking. I had no idea he bore such anger against me. I could not speak. I did not know what to say. I sat on a chair in the living room, physically paralyzed. I did not move—not for a long time. My mother went to bed, either impervious or preferring to deny the quarrel that was exploding around her. Jean-Pierre left the next morning without speaking to me.

We saw each other again nine months later because my mother had become ill and had moved to a nursing home. Once again, we fought. We were both staying at my parents' flat. This time, my brother accused me of a social infraction that was so slight I did not even remember it. I had apparently neglected to include him at a dinner a few days earlier with friends from Hong Kong. His concern was very out of character. I had no idea he had any interest in going to the dinner with my friends. But his anger had been triggered and he was unleashing it in full force.

After that, we met rarely. When we did, we talked about the weather, and about my mother. I tried not to visit Paulette when he was scheduled to be in London. Because I didn't know how to deal with him, because I was never sure whether another explosion was in the cards, I avoided him. For years after we buried our father, the night of his funeral remained vivid in my mind. I could still feel the seething resentment from Jean-Pierre, the passion in his voice, the look of hatred in his eyes. It frightened me. But equally sobering is that, while I was the target of his fury, I wonder whether his anger was in fact strictly at me. I think his rage extends way beyond me, that it is deeper and broader. He is like a wounded animal that lashes out at everything that touches him.

Jean-Pierre still lives in Majorca. He has not worked in years. After more than twenty-five years, Anik, who had eventually divorced the Canadian, gave up waiting for a commitment from him, and they no longer see each other.

When I asked him once what he did with his time, he told me he reads the newspaper. I have a mental image of him walking from his apartment every morning to the town center to buy *Le Monde and The Financial Times*. It would make sense to him to read about politics in French and to keep up with business in English. I'll bet he stops at the same café every day to drink two cups of extra-strong espresso. Then he heads home, walking at his now habitual slow gait, perhaps stopping for groceries or a loaf of bread. He bought the apartment, which is minutes away from the beach, because he likes being close to the water. But he never goes to the beach anymore. He does not like the sun or the sand, and he has developed an aversion to tourists. Instead, he sits on his spacious deck, hour after hour, admiring the ocean from afar. He used to like elaborate dishes, heavy in spices and sauces. But no more. He now lives on boiled rice, pasta and steamed vegetables.

Twice a month, Jean-Pierre has dinner with Steve Afif, Edith's eldest son. Edith died of a stroke and is buried in Majorca. Steve's brother Allan, who lives in London and with whom Jean-Pierre stayed when he visited my mother, travels to Majorca regularly and the three get together. Perhaps it is because of, or perhaps in spite of, Jean-Pierre's relationship with their mother, but strangely, the three men are like brothers.

Jean-Pierre must know a few other people. He must socialize occasionally. But he is basically a hermit. He makes phone calls from pay phones because he claims his home phone is tapped, and he still tells outrageous, nonsensical stories to the few who will listen. He travels occasionally, sometimes to Paris to see our cousins, but most often he used to go to London to see our mother before she died in March of 2005. True to his word, he never once assumed any responsibility for her or her financial affairs.

Paulette sometimes asked me if I would stay in touch with Jean-Pierre after her death. Sadly, at the time I thought probably not, but in fact, since her death my brother and I have stayed in touch by phone fairly regularly. When I was diagnosed with a brain tumor in March 2009, he began to call me more often, though our conversations are always brief and impersonal. In a strange way, I do love him, but I don't know him. I don't know if anyone does. It saddens me that he still cannot deal with his past or put his rage to rest. Like Anik, I have finally stopped reaching out. I no longer wait or hope for his affection.

18

Tony, Displacement as Opportunity

*A*ll of my moves to foreign places, of course, had a major impact on my life. During the unhappy and lonely times of my life when I felt like a stranger without a home, I often thought of my father and tried to see life the way I thought he would have seen it.

All those years ago, while we were confined under house arrest in Cairo, my father had put on a happy face for us. He had kept me busy and taken my mind off the daily stresses we faced. In the mornings I got up, had breakfast, took a bath, and then Tony would appear and say, "This morning we will type." I thought being with my father was a great way to spend time, and I have always been glad that he taught me typing. I did everything Tony said—and, of course, Jean-Pierre did nothing Tony said.

Everything my father did had to be done right. I admired this trait in him. If he was writing something, he wrote a draft and rewrote it. When I got older, I proofed his writing. He was meticulous about his written words. This priority could have originated with his work with messages at Marconi Cable & Wireless. He made a kind of game out of striving for perfection. After my parents retired in London, Tony took a special interest in shopping for food. He regularly took three different buses just to buy the perfect fruit. He would gladly travel one hour each way if that was what it took to find the best. In England, good apples were especially important to him, and to this day, apples remind me of Tony's quest for perfection.

As I grew older, I realized how much Tony had quietly endured in his life. I realized that he had known long in advance that we would eventually have to leave Egypt, and he must have been terrified to think of his children having no passports. As a young man, he hadn't needed to give much thought to passports. After all, his father had managed fine without a passport. However, the 1952 overthrow, abdication and exile of the ruling Mohammed Ali Dynasty brought profound changes to Egypt. Suddenly, lacking a passport was a very big deal.

I know that, as a Christian with a Jewish wife among Muslims, my father had always felt discriminated against in Egypt, though he never complained. Before our house arrest, the Egyptian government had begun to accuse my father of disloyalty. At Marconi Cable & Wireless, he translated cables for the British government. Suddenly, he was accused of spying. He, in fact, was turning over information to the British embassy to which it had no other access. Was this spying? This seems like a strained use of the term. It was also true that he was very loyal to the British, and he was not loyal to the Egyptians. They were Muslims. They did not like us. We were different from them. The implications of these developments must have cost my father some sleepless nights, but he tried not to let on.

After our traumatic departure from Cairo in 1956, Tony never waxed nostalgic. He never talked about going back to Egypt to live, even though it was his home, and even though he had left his mother behind when we were exiled.

Once, on a boat trip between England and Hong Kong, we learned she was ill. We left the boat during a port call in Egypt to see her in the hospital. This was daring because we did not have visas, and we had to lie to the immigration officials. As it turned out, we were quite lucky to have escaped, for the Egyptian officials were aware they had been lied to, and they were looking for us when we returned to port. We were ordered never to return to Egypt.

We made it to the hospital, where Tony's mother looked frail and old. It was clear she was near the end of her life. He was deeply grieved, for they both knew they would never see each other again. About six months after we returned to Hong Kong from England, Tony received a letter telling him that his mother had died. He cried often, and he wore a black tie for a year as a sign of respect and mourning. I am not sure whether the black tie was a Greek or an Egyptian custom, but it signaled Tony's love for his mother, and his regret that she had died without his being there.

My father was loyal to those he loved, and he took it hard when he lost them. I recall how, once, when he was visiting me during the Vietnam War, we went to a restaurant in Saigon. A man walked in and recognized Tony. They hugged each other, laughed and cried. Apparently, he was someone who, like us, had been thrown out of Egypt. He was Jewish, and he had since become like Tony, a man without a true home. He had lived in Paris, then London, and then Saigon. After their meeting in the restaurant, my father and this once-lost friend stayed in touch until Tony died.

Despite the high personal cost of his displacement from home, friends and family, Tony ultimately saw exile as an opportunity to move forward, and he was going to seize it. He viewed change as exciting, while my mother looked on it as disaster. In my own life, I struggled to see unwelcome, frightening changes the way Tony did and not the way my mother did. I tried never to feel too tied to any one place, but still to remember to look for the best aspects of the places where I found myself. Usually, I succeeded. I made an effort to teach my father's attitude to my own children, but they had minds of their own. My daughter hated moving around, and my son loved it.

If you had asked Tony, he would have told you that exile dramatically improved his life. He would never have been successful or accepted in Egypt. After he left Cairo, he said, there was one bad year. However, from then on, his life only got better. In the late 1960s when he told me this, I hoped I would be able to say the same about my own life one day, but at the time all I could think was that I felt like a homeless, lonely wanderer.

19

Paulette,
Contrary Love
1977-2005

*M*y mother never stopped feeling like an outsider. All
her life, she called herself une étrangère, a stranger.
My mother said none of the countries where she had lived after
Egypt were her countries, but some were more comfortable than
others. At the end of her life, she liked England because she had
free medical care, free medications and money in the bank. For
one surgery she complained she had been required to wait too
long, but aside from that, she was comfortable. It was as if her
first move to London had faded from her memory as one of the
most wrenching times of her life.

Rents were expensive in London. Tony had saved for two
decades in Hong Kong, so they had been able to pay cash for a
house in Putney, a nice middle-class, suburban London home. My
father never had a credit card and never wanted debt. He liked the
debit card. Their golden years were happy ones. They visited me in
Paris, and once a year they went to the south of France. My mother

traveled to Australia twice to see her sisters. Unfortunately, Paulette began to show signs of macular degeneration around 1977, at first only in one eye. But eventually both eyes were involved, and she couldn't read anymore. Her condition progressed very slowly, but in the end she had extremely low vision. I think reading was the hardest thing for her to lose. Her condition increased her sense of isolation, especially after Tony died. She was quite distraught, and she went to a lot of doctors, but they kept telling her there was nothing they could do.

When Tony died in 1997, the doctor said he believed Paulette wouldn't live much longer, but in fact she lived another eight years. Like Jean-Pierre, she had reacted very badly to Tony's death. She took Jean-Pierre's side in the fury he unleashed at me at my father's funeral. To make matters worse, the day after Tony's funeral, my mother couldn't even remember the funeral. She accused me of having forgotten to take her. Painful things were said that day, on all sides, but eventually we all moved on.

My mother's vision eventually deteriorated to the point where she couldn't put a key in the door or turn on the stove by herself. She had to make arrangements with the neighbors to let her into her own home. I wanted her to move into an assisted living facility, but she and Jean-Pierre fought against me.

One time I called Paulette and could not reach her. I phoned the caretaker of her building. I had given him a key just in case something like this might happen but, meanwhile, Jean-Pierre had confiscated it for fear someone might misuse it. The caretaker had to break a window to get into her apartment to see if she was okay. She wasn't home. Ten minutes later, she and a friend returned from an outing, and she called me long-distance, angry at me for causing a disturbance.

Without Tony, it was just a matter of time until a crisis developed. I said, "How are you going to continue to live here?" I suggested that Jean-Pierre could come and live with her, because I could not. My son was still in college, I was divorced, and I had no money. I told her she would have to go to a nursing home. When Paulette was stressed, she would call me in the U. S. and ask me to come over for the day, as if I were somewhere close by. Jean-Pierre and I came up with a solution. We each agreed to visit her every three months, but not at the same time, so she would have one of us there at least every six weeks or so.

Ultimately, she admitted she couldn't stay home alone anymore. She had a slip at night and there was nobody to call. She fell many times. I went to London and found a nursing home that seemed acceptable to her and to me. That is where she went in the summer of 1998. Jean-Pierre and I still visited every three months, and I talked to her on the phone every day. These were five- or ten-minute conversations. She complained about the home and about the people who worked there. However, her friends came to see her, and after a while she said that Tony came and talked to her during the night. After that, she was much better.

As my mother's health declined, she'd often say, "It's time for me to die; why don't you kill me?" She was agreeable only when somebody she liked came to see her. Unlike my father's family, who liked to talk about the good old days, my mother didn't enjoy talking about the past. For my mother and her side of the family, there were no good old days. They were all terrible. Toward the end of Paulette's life, I tried to ascertain her wishes, and I would ask her, "What do you want me to do with you when you die?" She said, "I want you to throw me away." Finally, I got out of her that she wanted to be buried in a Jewish cemetery.

She never went to the synagogue, but throughout much of her life she had followed kosher laws. After her own mother died, however, she came up with some amusing compromises. She argued, for instance, that eating ham was okay if it was sliced very thin.

When Paulette's health began to deteriorate seriously, and after she had decided about her burial, I went to the synagogue to meet the director. I asked if he would visit her. He did. During the Jewish holidays, someone would come and pray over her. Despite medical advice, she continued to smoke, and she encouraged me to smoke too. Paulette was both charming and impossible.

I was in California in March 2005 when I received the news that she had died. Someone from the Jewish community said, "We'll wash her tonight and bury her tomorrow."

I said, "No, wait. I have to get there." They gave me forty-eight hours.

Her funeral hit me hard. I found it difficult to accept that my mother, such a daily presence in my life, was gone.

Paulette was a strong woman. She was quite dominating. I found her very difficult. Everything I wanted, she did not want for me. I wanted to swim; she thought that would mess up my hair. I desperately wanted an education; she denied that I needed one. I wanted to be a journalist; she declared it to be a vulgar profession. Paulette doted on her own personal appearance, and I didn't care about that. I was either too fat or too skinny. I was never right.

I'm sure at times in my life I was jealous and resentful that she spoiled Jean-Pierre and gave him all the things that I had wanted—in particular, a university education. But in the end, as she was laid to rest in London, I could only think how much I loved her, and how much I would miss her.

20

Reflections on Displacement

With my parents gone, I thought about their lives and a time, years earlier, when I had almost lost them. It happened in their suburban London apartment complex. That event helped me put their displacement and my own exile into context.

My thoughts focused on a specific day when gas from an antiquated pipe had been leaking slowly—too slowly for anyone to notice. On that Monday afternoon in the dead of winter, when the air in London turns frigid, gas usage rose to its peak. As the leak intensified, gas began to move silently throughout a building, to fill every space until it met with a spark—someone's afternoon tea kettle set on the stove, perhaps. The resultant explosion shattered everything in its path. My parents' apartment shook violently, and then stood still for a terrifying few seconds before giving a final shudder. Windows, unable to withstand the pressure, disgorged panes of glass that shattered on contact with walls and furniture before disintegrating into thousands of fine shards and splinters spread over the floor.

The building adjoining theirs took the full brunt of the fury. Flames poured out of windows and doors, and within minutes the structure was engulfed in fire. There was no time to evacuate the residents who were home at the time. Two war widows, diminutive white-haired ladies with heavily wrinkled, weather-beaten faces, had shared an apartment in the building for decades. Both perished. Neighbors cried silently and bent their heads in respect when, hours later, an ambulance carried their covered bodies out on stretchers. The other residents of the buildings huddled in hallways on that dark London night and felt an added chill. The explosion brought memories of the Blitz, decades past but permanently etched in their collective memories.

My parents had lived in the apartment complex on the southwestern edge of London for several years since their return to England from Hong Kong in 1977. Because they were retired, and because they enjoyed walking, they had the time to meander through the well-tended grounds. Although they took little advantage of it, they had time to meet and greet their neighbors, many of whom were also past their prime. In the spring and summer, when the light in London remains radiant and shimmers late into the evening, as though trying to recompense Londoners for the long dark days of winter, my parents would stroll through the gardens, sit on the slatted wooden benches, and admire the profusion of flowers. But they paid little attention to their neighbors. They might nod at someone passing who greeted them with a "good morning," but that was the extent of their affability. And while their neighbors drew comfort and strength from each other on the night of the explosion, my parents found solace in their own company.

They did not have much in common with the other residents. For my parents, the catastrophe did not evoke memories of the Blitz. Instead, for them, the explosion recalled the terrifying day in 1952 when the Egyptian military engineered a coup d'état and, after overthrowing King Farouk, soldiers rampaged Cairo and burned as much as they could in their path.

In Cairo, our own building had been set aflame, and we had waited to see if the fire would reach us on our floor. In London at the time of the gas explosion, once again I stood with my parents on the balcony of a sixth-floor apartment, watching the flames creeping up the gray stone walls below, our eyes burning from the thick smoke rising into the air, and our ears assaulted by the noise of the inferno and the human commotion below. The fire miraculously burned itself out when it reached the second floor, leaving us relieved but drained.

Although it had been twenty-eight years since they had first landed in London—twenty-eight years since that momentous day in December 1956 when they had been forced to flee Egypt—my parents, like many of their contemporaries from Cairo and Alexandria, remained intellectually and emotionally removed from their physical surroundings. In their minds they lived in a remembered world that no longer existed and to which they could never return. They were suspended in time and place. The gas explosion brought home their emotional distance and disjointed sense of place. They watched the devastation, but they did so with a sense of detachment, lacking empathy for their neighbors. After all, this was not their home. They saw many of their neighbors leave in a large group a week later to attend the funeral of the two war widows. I asked them why they had not gone to the service.

"We didn't know them," my father replied, surprised that I was asking a question with an answer he clearly perceived as all too obvious.

My parents "knew" only people who, like themselves, were exiles from Egypt. And although my father was born Roman Catholic, he had married into a Jewish family and become acculturated to their ways. This, too, created a feeling of distance between him and his London neighbors.

Immigrants who leave their homes voluntarily in search of a better future often feel estranged in their new surroundings. But their displacement, unlike my parents', has usually been at least somewhat planned and voluntary. They have made a conscious choice, and they now must struggle to find their place and to create a sense of belonging within their adopted home. They invariably suffer through a period when they are not at home either in the old or in the new place. I have European friends who, during their first years of living in the United States, fantasize about an island in the Atlantic that would combine the qualities of the old and the new—in other words, create a sort of middle ground, a haven embodying the best of both worlds.

Over time, these immigrants adjust to their new environments, some more easily than others. The acculturation process is slow and subtle, bewildering and painful, but they have a safety net— they can always go home. After a while, they are astonished when they realize that a transformation has occurred. This realization might come in a flash, an overnight revelation.

One day, the immigrant realizes suddenly that she has changed. Something happens that would previously have made her stop and shake her head.

What once seemed strange is now commonplace and does not set off an alarm that jolts her nervous system. She realizes that her surroundings no longer feel alien and that the customs, language and manners that once seemed odd to her now appear familiar and unexceptional.

When I was still relatively new to the United States and living in Rockwall, Texas, I was startled when the woman behind the counter at the dry cleaners drawled, "Y'all come back." I was startled when tea in tall glasses full of ice cubes was served with meals. In my world, we drank wine with our meals, and we enjoyed hot tea, served in china cups, in the morning and in the afternoon. I was shocked again when an acquaintance asked what church we intended to join, and I was confused by the abundance of Christian denominations. A billboard on the highway I traversed daily featured a life-sized image of a minister who promised that prosperity would come to those who accepted Jesus. What kind of prosperity? I wondered. The sort that enabled everyone to live in the suburbs, in houses that looked alike, with the same kinds of cars parked in every driveway?

I found it ironic that in the United States, where I had been led to believe that individuality was prized, the homes I was invited into all looked identical, as did the hostesses. I was confused by the conformity. I was uncomfortable with people's easy familiarity. Everyone I met, from the cashier at the grocery store who called me by my first name to the teachers at my children's school who were surprisingly casual, seemed blandly informal. I was accustomed to relationships punctuated by formalities and rituals. In the United States, I had no idea how to tell the difference between genuine friendliness and polite courtesy, and I was unsure how to interpret the flatness of tone and the absence of passion in conversations lacking animation.

Years later, while writing my master's thesis, I read the memoirs of Edward Said, the prominent Palestinian activist whose family was displaced from their home in 1948 when the state of Israel was created, and who spent his childhood in Cairo and Beirut before settling in the United States. I was struck by his comment that the Americans he met "seemed less emotional, with little interest in articulating their attitudes and reactions." Said found American society to be so extraordinarily homogenized that it "seemed to limit the complex intercourse of daily life to an unreflective minimum in which memory has no role."[2] In contrast, he felt that his own memories were directing his life.

My memories were alive in me, but nevertheless, while driving home one day six months or so after I had moved to Dallas, I realized that the evangelist's billboard no longer made the same impression on me. I had started to say "sure thing" to the dry cleaner who always invited me to come back.

I was changing.

Unlike my parents, who had been forced to leave their homeland, I had made a somewhat reluctant but nevertheless conscious choice to move to the United States. The adjustment to my new environment was therefore somewhat easier. But while I became reconciled to my surroundings, I continued to live in a sort of no-man's land, with one foot in the present and another in the past. I could appreciate both worlds.

My parents, like their contemporaries, lived strictly in the past. Their move had not been voluntary and their transition was more tenuous, more difficult and elusive. Many exiles like my parents live in limbo, in a state of permanent disorientation. They cannot go forward, but neither can they go back. It is as though the shock of their ejection from their home has paralyzed them. They exist in a perpetual state of transit, unable even to conceive of an alternative condition.

The conventional wisdom that "time heals" is a fallacy. I agree with Edward Said, who suggests that time deepens wounds. "The fact that I live in New York with a sense of provisionality," he writes, "despite thirty-seven years of residence here accentuates the disorientation that has accrued in me, rather than the advantages."[3] In other words, if you don't adapt quickly, if you don't feel at home in a relatively short period of time, your new home looks more alien daily and you feel increasingly estranged. You remain suspended in time and place.

Andre Aciman, a Jew displaced from Egypt in the 1950s, compares exile to love: "Exile, like love, is not just a condition of pain; it's a condition of deceit. Or put it another way: exiles can be supremely mobile, and they can be totally dislodged from their original orbit, but in this jittery state of transience, they are thoroughly stationary—no less stationary than those displaced Europeans perpetually awaiting letters of transit in the film *Casablanca*. They are never really in Casablanca, but they are not going anywhere either. They are in permanent transience." [4]

Like Said, Aciman contends that it is "precisely because you have no roots that you don't budge, that you fear change, that you'll build on anything rather than look for land. An exile is not just someone who has lost his home; it is someone who can't find another, who can't think of another. Some no longer even know what home means." [5] Recalling his early years in the Middle East and the United States, after his family had been exiled from Palestine, Said laments, "I may have envied friends whose language was one or the other, or who had lived in the same place all their lives, or who had done well in accepted ways, or who truly belonged, but I do not recall ever thinking that any of that was possible for me." [6]

Displacement is not an unusual phenomenon. Famine once forced Irish farmers to abandon their land for more fertile ground in America. Civil wars in Africa, Asia, South and Central America have occasioned massive forced movements of populations. Millions of Jews fled Europe in World War II. Families displaced from Palestine in 1948 continued to live in limbo six decades later in refugee camps in Lebanon and Jordan. Thousands who fled the revolutions in Hungary and in Cuba in the mid-1950s saw their hopes for a return home dwindle and disappear. Many more left the former Yugoslavia when civil war broke out in the 1990s. More recently, British ranchers in the former Rhodesia were sent packing by a new generation of African leaders, and Iraqi families have sought shelter in neighboring countries from the U.S.-led war.

In recent years, images of diaspora have become ubiquitous on television news programs. Almost daily, we see displaced men and women, their faces contorted with pain and fear, carrying bundles on their backs, balancing packages on their heads, pulling handcarts, or walking in processions through deserts, brush and forests. Viewers in Europe and the United States have become numb to this kind of human devastation, but each individual victim has a detailed story to tell.

The event that touched my family had its roots in Egypt in the revolution of 1952. Sinister, post-revolutionary rage simmered until 1956. Then, like the leaking gas in my parents' apartment, it ignited to engulf the foreign and Jewish populations. Since biblical times, Egypt had featured prominently in the Jewish psyche, but the saga was coming to a close.

The authors of *Juifs d'Egypte: Image et Textes*, published in Paris in 1984, remark how Egypt has always figured in Jewish consciousness. All fourteen of these writers, Jewish academicians either born in Egypt or resided there for extended periods of time, suggest that even in the days following the Exodus from Egypt, when the Jews wandered with Moses through the desert for forty years, they craved "the onions, the pickles and the roast meats they had enjoyed on the banks of the Nile. . . . It took no less than the gigantic grapes, the milk and the honey of the Promised Land" to appease them, "and even then, they could not forget the good produce emanating from the earth of the pharaohs." [7]

Egypt, rich in wheat, was the Middle Eastern breadbasket, the land to which Jews in Canaan had always turned when they were hungry; it had always been a promised land, a sort of America without the obstacle of an ocean to traverse.

In 1492, when Spain forced its Jewish population either to convert to Christianity or leave the country, the displaced Sephardim settled in North Africa, including Egypt. By the sixteenth century, when the Turks occupied Egypt, Jews had risen to prominence as the handlers of the Ottoman Empire's finances and collectors of its taxes. In 1557, Hebrew texts made their debut in another language, Arabic, first in Cairo, and five years later in Alexandria. Egypt's successive occupiers and monarchs encouraged the Jewish community to grow and flourish. By 1897, Egypt's Jewish population totaled over twenty-five thousand out of a population of nine million. By 1917, there were nearly sixty thousand Jews in a country of thirteen million. Not only were they growing in numbers, but their power and prosperity were expanding. Jews controlled many of the banks, owned department stores, and handled most of the country's trade. They had become Egypt's intellectual and financial elite.

However, by late 1956 and continuing for about a decade, as many as one hundred thousand of these Jews were forced to leave Egypt, where many had lived for generations, some families for centuries. Still, they often carried passports of countries they had never visited rather than papers of citizenship of the land over which they felt a strong sense of ownership. These passports were their security, their way out if the need arose.

One never knew what turns a life could suddenly take, and life for Jews in the middle of the twentieth century had been anything but reassuring. Since 1948 and the establishment of Israel, Egyptians had looked with growing skepticism at the Jewish community. Jews were sometimes respected and appreciated, sometimes merely tolerated, but often resented and ostracized. By the 1950s, the national climate had soured and was ripe for rapid and radical change. With the overthrow of King Farouk in 1952 and the rapid ascendancy of Colonel Gamal Abdel Nasser, Egypt shifted its allegiance from the Franco-British-American sphere of influence and threw in its lot with the Soviet Union. The reign begun with Mohamed Ali in 1805 came to an abrupt and violent end. The personal and professional lives of Jews in Egypt began to unravel.

In 1956, when Nasser nationalized the Suez Canal and a joint British, French, and Israeli military expedition attacked Egypt, the last page of the history book of the Jews in Egypt had been written. Their days and nights were filled with tension and terror. Most members of the foreign and Jewish communities stayed home, barricading themselves in their apartments and relying on their servants for food and morsels of news from the outside world. Some, like my family, were put under house arrest. But despite the unfortunate turn of events, the Jewish community remained hopeful. That had always been their attitude. Few would allow themselves to make plans for an exodus. They had ridden rough waves before and had always landed safely. But this time, the tide was running powerfully against them.

The British, French, and Americans were no longer welcome in Egypt. Jewish-owned assets were confiscated and Jews were not allowed to hold jobs or to own businesses or property. These developments were tantamount to expulsion. Only a few, too elderly or feeble to travel, chose to remain in Cairo and Alexandria. The remainder sought refuge in any country that would grant them entry.

My immediate family was relatively lucky. We were expelled, but we had a place to go. My aunt and uncle and their two children were given a temporary visa by the French. They lived in Paris, spending hours daily at French government offices—at a United Nations office for displaced people, at the headquarters of the Jewish refugee organization—desperately seeking admission to a country where they could stay permanently. A year elapsed before they were told they could move to Australia. They were both relieved and disturbed. Australia was so far away, so remote, so unknown.

Our friends the Galantes, who had lost an immense fortune acquired over several generations in Cairo and whose daughter Vivianne was my close friend, went to Rio de Janeiro. "Where is that?" someone asked. "It is in Brazil." People nodded. They heard the word *Brazil*, but they could not fathom living there. We thought it seemed far away, but then we remembered that without a home, we had no real measure for *far* or *near*.

Years later, watching a production of *Fiddler on the Roof,* I identified with the exiled character in the play who announced he was moving to Madagascar. "Madagascar!" his friend exclaimed. "That's so far."

The man without a home replies, "Far from what?" [8]

The newly displaced Egyptian Jews scattered across the world to London, Paris and Milan, to Melbourne, Montreal and New York. They clustered in the same neighborhoods, invariably ignoring and perhaps genuinely oblivious to their new surroundings, encouraging their children to marry each other, struggling to protect their customs and culture, and continuing to speak French with a distinct lilt, replete with Middle Eastern idioms, and marked by an occasional Arabic phrase. And although many were fluent in English, Italian, and a plethora of other languages, their Middle Eastern accent was their identity card, a badge that defined them, that helped them recognize one another, and that pointed to their common history and culture. Religion was important, but what they clung to tightest were family, friends and familiarity.

One gathering at the home of friends in London in early 1957 is forever fixed in my memory. Familiar foods were spread on the table. The conversation was loud and carried on in multiple languages, and bright lights and warm air graced the room. The atmosphere was almost joyous. In part, we were elated at having the nightmare behind us and having a place to land. We also felt buoyed by our mutual sense of impermanence, as though we were only on vacation from our homes. Nothing felt real. Not the furnished rooms in which we were all living. Not the inhospitable city of London that was still struggling to recover from the devastation of World War II. Not the daily efforts to find jobs, to survive in schools where instruction was in English, a language none of us spoke. Not the struggle to cope with an uncomfortable and alien climate. Because everything seemed so unreal, it was easy not to think long-term and to live as though tomorrow would bring a welcome return to normalcy.

Hardly anyone tried to learn English. My mother refused even to acknowledge the peculiar delineations of English currency, which back then counted four farthings to the penny, twelve pennies to the shilling, twenty shillings to the pound, and twenty-one shillings to the guinea. The children and teenagers clung to one another. We would go to the movies on Saturday afternoons, but otherwise we ventured only to school and to one another's homes. Like our adult relatives, we felt numb to our surroundings, uninterested in the world around us. Perhaps we could not conceive, or allow ourselves to believe, that this city could become our permanent home. I became a part of a little clique with a boy named Alan, who had played with me in the sandbox in Cairo when we were toddlers, and his brother Steve, who like my brother, was five years older than we were.

Sometimes we went to the movies (called the "pictures" back then) at the Odeon Theatre on High Street Kensington on Saturday afternoons. Once, when we were waiting in the packed theatre for the film to start, two rough looking young men asked us to move. They wanted our seats. When we refused, they started yelling anti-Semitic insults. The four of us were paralyzed in shock. We were too self-conscious and stunned to move. We had not thought that anti-Semitism existed outside of Arab countries. The four of us learned that afternoon that we would have to deal with prejudice, ignorance and anger wherever we lived. Our sense of exile was reinforced that afternoon and although we did not discuss it—in retrospect, I realize we did not know how to discuss it—we realized that, at least at some level, we would always feel like outsiders. Where we lived was irrelevant and always would be. Home was everywhere but nowhere.

Alan still lives in London, in the same neighborhood where his family rented an apartment in the 1950s. His English is fluent but his accent is unchanged. His wife is Israeli, and despite making London his home for close to fifty years, he remains a foreigner, a private person who keeps his own counsel. Steve and my brother both live in Spain. They speak a heavily accented, albeit fluent Spanish, and they, too, keep to themselves. They have never felt at home, regardless of where they have chosen to live.

Far removed from the chaos of the Cairo streets, from the beauty of the Alexandrian coastline and the serenity of the Sahara, Egyptian Jews continue to dream of these places, to cherish them in their minds and souls, and to ignore the sad fact that the home they remember exists today only in their memories. Aciman suggests that exiles suffer from a common, pervasive ailment that he characterizes as "compulsive retrospection."

In *Juifs d'Egypte* we are reminded that after their most recent diaspora from Egypt, the Jews, now dispersed throughout the world, remain aware of the dangers of layering their memories with false or exaggerated reminiscences. Still, they "keep intact the hours of their Egyptian childhoods which they recollect with delight and repeat to the envy of others." Their Egypt has vividly endured in their individual and collective recollections.

The last page of the Egyptian-Jewish saga may have been written in 1956, but my family and most of their friends have kept the book open, the pages frozen in time. Turning the page would bring unwanted closure, tantamount to rejecting the past, to burying the body, to letting go the animate soul. But, for them, to live in and savor the past requires a distance from the present, a rejection and a disregard for current surroundings. Part of the comfort of living in the past, I believe, is that we don't have to explain ourselves; we don't have to affix some sort of terminus to our history. Edward Said recalls that his biggest challenge, when he first came to America to attend high school, was not knowing how to present and explain himself. "Nationality, background, real origins, and past actions all seemed to be the source of my problem," he writes. "So beginning in America I resolved to live as if I were a simple, transparent soul and not to speak about my family or origins, except as required, and then, very sparingly."

Only with one another could the Jews of Egypt not have to explain themselves. Only with one another would they keep alive the memories of an exuberant life in bustling metropolises that were radiant in the sun, resonating with life, reverberating with noise and rife with odors. With whom else could they spend boisterous evenings, talking as loudly as they pleased, switching languages with the ease and speed of a magician pulling ribbons and rabbits out of a hat, interrupting with evident enjoyment, debating issues with the zeal of professional politicians and laughing at stories that they embellished in every retelling?

I do not think that my parents tried to cling to their past lives in Egypt nearly as much as they tried to keep some of their old ways and customs, especially when it came to food. They sought out people with similar backgrounds. My parents' friends had names like Cohen and Levy, Curiel and Cicurel, Gallante, Misrahi and Harari, Safdieh and Setton, de Botton and Afif. They talked on the phone, gathered in one another's homes, played cards, and talked of the past. They kept in touch with Egyptian Jews in other cities and shared every morsel of news they had gleaned. The same stories were told and retold. The people sought comfort in their collective nostalgia, and they rarely ventured outside their tight-knit community, where they felt safe and where outsiders were not welcome. They prepared elaborate meals, set tables laden with *konafas, menenas and sambousseks.* For special occasions, my parents and their friends would scour grocery stores in Arab neighborhoods of the cities where they lived, looking for the ingredients needed to make *molokheia,* a sinewy green soup, *foul meddames* and other familiar dishes.

My parents' circle—*les amis* they called themselves—took food very seriously. Buying the right produce from the right source mattered. My father, even late in his life when he walked with difficulty and tired easily, rode the bus from Putney in southwest London into Knightsbridge, where he boarded a second bus to the city's northern suburbs. There he had found a Greek greengrocer in Hampstead who had grown up in Monsourrah, the provincial Egyptian town where my father was born. The man, my father decided, clearly could be trusted to sell quality fruits and vegetables. The trip there and back could take as long as two hours, but my father felt it was worth the effort. He would come home laden with zucchini, eggplants, artichokes, okra and tangerines. There were greengrocers closer to home, but they were English or Irish. "What did they know about fruits and vegetables?" my father asked rhetorically, as he struggled to preserve at least a culinary semblance of home. Foreign food was symbolic of change, and change is anathema to exiles and refugees. It reminds them of their loss and of the vulnerability of what remains.

Aciman complains: "I hate it when stores change names, the way I hate any change of season, not because I like winter more than spring, or because I like [the] old store . . . better than [the] new . . . but because . . . any change reminds me of how imperfectly I've connected. . . . It reminds me of the thing I fear most: that my feet are never quite solidly on the ground, but also that the soil under me is equally weak, that the graft didn't take. In the disappearance of small things, I read the tokens of my own dislocation, of my own transiency."

Recently, I came across a newspaper article by a columnist in Texas writing about selling the home of his deceased parents. He had hoped his children would want some of their grandparents' furniture, but he realized that these objects meant nothing to them and would be simply a burden. The children of the Jewish Egyptian diaspora are not burdened by such possessions—these were taken from them long ago—but by memories that continue to shape our identities, regardless of the countries we have chosen to call home.

21

Little Black Books

W hen I was around ten years old, my father brought home two miniature black books. He held them on his open palm, handling them like fragile treasures. They had hard covers embossed with an elaborate, golden seal. Most thrilling was the narrow slit cut across the bottom of each book. On one of them was my name, written in a fancy script in jet black ink: "Miss Micheline Trigaci." I was unaccustomed to being called "Miss," so the word made me feel very grown-up and important. The other book belonged to my brother, Jean-Pierre.

We were allowed to look at them and touch them, but only briefly and gingerly. They were very important documents, my father told us. After a few minutes, he took them away and hid them in the top right-hand drawer of his bureau. That is also where he kept his money, tucked under shelf-lining paper, with his neatly folded undershirts lying on top, providing a foil for would-be thieves.

The books were exciting, but their significance escaped me. I don't think Jean-Pierre, despite being five years older, understood either. Two years later, when our world was turned upside down, my father and mother kept muttering, "Thank God the children have passports." But still I did not make the connection between their sense of relief and the little black books that had so thrilled me when I first looked at them.

A decade had passed, years after our world had been torn asunder, before I finally started to put the pieces together. The little black books, the passports that had been both our salvation and the reason for our exile from Egypt, were about to expire. I was twenty years old and living in New York when Tony wrote me a letter reminding me to renew my passport. Before leaving Hong Kong, he had given me an envelope with my birth certificate and other documents. I had not bothered ever to open the envelope, so I took the whole thing along with me that morning to the British Consulate in midtown Manhattan.

I handed my passport and the documents to the man behind the desk. He looked at them, frowned, stared at them some more, and then disappeared into a back room. Within a few minutes, he reappeared and invited me into an office where an Englishman in a dark suit—some sort of consular officer—was sitting behind a large wooden desk.

"How did you get this?" he asked, pointing at the document Tony had included in the envelope.

"My father gave it to me. He said I might need it to renew my passport."

"Who is your father? What does he do? Where does he live?"

I gave him my father's name and told him that he worked for the telegraph company in Hong Kong, but that he used to have a similar job in Cairo.

"Ah, Cairo!" the man said. "Did you leave in 1956?"

"Yes, we did."

"That explains it," the consular office said.

"Explains what?"

The consular officer did not answer.

The man clearly knew something I didn't know. I left the consulate with my new passport in hand, but feeling unsettled. I pulled out the document that had so interested the consular officer and discovered it was a naturalization certificate. At the bottom there was a typed statement, with a seal embossed over it, saying the naturalization had occurred by "special circumstance." I kept remembering the refrain—"now that the children have passports"— that I had heard so often in Cairo and in the months following our expulsion. I remembered vividly how my father had handled the little black books so carefully the day he brought them home.

Months passed before I got back to Hong Kong and was able to quiz Tony about what had happened.

"The man at the consulate office in New York City was very mysterious," I told him. "He knew something I didn't know. They asked me if I was British by birth or by naturalization, and I didn't know the answer. I was sure I wasn't British by birth, because I remember some of what you said when you brought those passports home. But how could we have been naturalized when we were in Egypt? Then I gave the man the papers you had given me and that seemed to satisfy him, but I think there was something funny going on."

As a teenager, I had been curious about my family's history. I had wanted to know where my grandparents and parents came from, and how they had ended up in Cairo. Both Tony and Paulette would tell me to worry about today and tomorrow. What happened in the past wasn't interesting or relevant, they always said.

"The past is all about old people," Paulette would say. "They are mostly dead now, so why worry about them?"

But Tony, having finally decided at least partially to explain the passport puzzle, started talking about his family. My paternal grandfather was Maltese and therefore entitled to a British passport. So were his children and their spouses. But the privilege did not extend to his grandchildren. Consequently, Tony had a British passport and so did Paulette. But Jean-Pierre and I were out of the loop. The Egyptian government rarely gave citizenship to the children of foreigners, and certainly not if their mothers were Jews. Jean-Pierre and I were therefore born stateless—people without a country, without identification, and without travel documents.

"If I hadn't been able to secure the passports, and we had been forced to leave Egypt, we would have had to leave you behind," Tony explained.

I thought about that for a minute. I could not think it through. If Paulette and Tony, and our uncles and aunts, had left Cairo that December morning without us, Jean-Pierre and I would have become street children. It was too horrifying a thought to contemplate.

Tony spoke for the first time to me then about years of anguish, about years when political turmoil threatened to force him and Paulette out of Egypt. He recalled the dark days during the Israeli War of Independence in 1948 and the panic that had spread through the foreign community during the Egyptian Revolution of 1952.

"I had to do something," Tony told me as he seemed to relive those last days in Cairo. His tone was passionate. The years might have gone by, but his emotions were as vivid as when the events were unfolding.

"I wrote a letter to the Queen and told her of our predicament. I told her that my father had worked for her government, and that I worked for her government, and so did your two uncles. I explained that I was a loyal subject and in a terrible quandary. I begged for her help.

"I got a call from the British Embassy a couple of months later, and they agreed to make an exception for you and Jean-Pierre. They gave both of you British passports. That's why the consular officer in New York was so taken aback. It is rare for people to become British by special circumstance."

"Wow," I said. "That was it? That's all you had to do? Write a letter? To the Queen? And she made it happen?"

Tony beamed at me. His tone had changed. The fear and the emotion that had been so visceral were gone.

"It took time. It had to go through Parliament."

"Through Parliament!"

"That's what the 'special circumstances' phrase means on your naturalization papers," he said. "Once you and Jean-Pierre got passports, I stopped being so anxious. Now I knew that if we had to leave, we'd all leave together."

I was astounded. The first part of the story sounded so real, so poignant. The second part was implausible, like a fairy tale with a happy ending. It did not make sense. If that was all there was to it, why had my parents made such a big secret of it all? I felt the same uneasiness I had experienced when I had left the British Consulate months earlier. Something was still missing.

"Why did we have to leave?" I asked him. I had asked the same question many times before, but I'd never received a satisfactory answer.

"You know the answer. Your mother is Jewish."

"But her sister and brother-in-law and all her cousins didn't have to leave, and they were all Jewish. They all stayed, and when they finally left, they took their things with them."

"It was better that we left," he said, growing quiet once again. That was his standard answer. "Look at Charlie. Five years in an Egyptian prison."

Two years after this conversation with my father, I was in London visiting his sister, my Aunt Alice. I had always been close to Alice. Since my mother was Jewish and I was raised Catholic, Alice was my "Catholic mother." And because she had no children, I was her surrogate daughter. I told her I was thinking about becoming a U.S. citizen. I was living in the United States and intended to make it my permanent home. She looked shocked.

"Have you told your father?" she asked.

"Yes, I mentioned it to him."

"What was his reaction?" Alice asked.

"He wanted to make sure I did not give up my British passport."

Alice sighed deeply. "And are you going to give it up?" she asked.

"Of course not," I said.

"After all that trouble, to give it up would be terrible," she said.

"What trouble?"

"The trouble your father had getting you and Jean-Pierre British passports."

"Oh, yes," I said. "He told me."

"He told you what?"

"That he had written to the Queen."

Alice looked exasperated. "And you believed that?" she asked, shaking her head at me as if I were an imbecile.

I remembered the skepticism I had felt at the time, my sense that Tony had left out a lot of important pieces of the story.

Alice filled in all the missing details. At the time when Tony got us passports, she had guessed the truth, she told me. She had confronted him because she feared the consequences of his decision. He had indeed written to the Queen, whose secretary had sent the letter on to the British Embassy in Cairo. That part was true. My father had been invited to the embassy, but in place of the fairy tale he had recounted to me, Alice told me how the embassy official had asked him what he would be willing to do in return for the passports he was seeking. Before Tony could collect his thoughts, the official had prompted him with the correct answer.

"You have all the code books, don't you?" he asked my father.

"Yes, I do," Tony answered.

The quid pro quo was that Tony would transcribe the diplomatic documents sent to the Egyptian government—back then, they all went through the telegraph office—decode them, and hand them over to embassy officials. The man warned that if my father were to be apprehended, he risked being imprisoned. The British government would not come to his rescue.

For four years, Tony transcribed and decoded messages. Several days a week, he left his office and walked eight blocks to "drop points" near the British Embassy where he would casually leave that day's messages. He must have decided from the beginning that the less Paulette knew, the better, because he had kept his activities secret even from her. Two years into that assignment, he handed us our passports, but he continued the decoding for two more years.

What he did not know during those two months of our house arrest, and the questions he did not talk to us about, concerned how much the Egyptian government knew. Had they picked on us alone, or were they rounding up everyone with British passports? Or were they rounding up all the Jews? Why had Charlie been arrested? Was he doing the same thing as Tony? Those were the questions that tortured my father while he played cards and danced with us in our home in Cairo before the soldiers came.

Thanks to aunt Alice, all of the pieces started to fall into place for me. The Egyptians must have known what both Tony and Charlie were doing, even though the two men clearly had not confided in each other. I don't know why they chose to arrest Charlie and expel us. Perhaps it was just the luck of the draw.

The next time I was in Hong Kong, I waited for Paulette to go to bed and for Tony to settle down to his nightly game of solitaire. I told him that Alice had helped me fill the gaps and better understand the mysterious story that he had told me about our passports. He looked startled, but only for a second. Then he laughed. It was a dry, forced laugh.

"Your aunt Alice," he said, shaking his head. "She has a vivid imagination. It's all those years of reading novels. She should have had children to keep her busy."

I always got startled looks whenever I renewed my British passport. But I learned to be prepared. What I will never know is whether Alice was right. "It is because of the passports," she had exclaimed to Tony in the airport lounge on the day we left Cairo. Ironically, the passports that Tony had so courageously struggled to obtain—the documents that were intended to keep my brother and me from being without a country—turned out to initiate a long chain of events that dispersed our whole family throughout different parts of the world and brought me, finally, here, to Austin, Texas.

22

Austin, Home at Last

*A*fter I retired, Robert and I planned a return trip to Egypt. I was really excited about the idea of returning for the first time in fifty years. I no longer had family there, but I wanted to see the house and hear what the people sounded like. I wanted to see the club where Jean-Pierre and I used to swim, where Paulette used to lounge in a chair alongside the pool, and where Tony used to pace back and forth in alarm at his son's swimming escapades.

A few weeks before we were scheduled to leave, I was diagnosed with brain cancer. I suppose now I will never be able to go. Nor will I ever return to England or France, most probably. After my mother died in 2005, I didn't renew my British passport. I didn't see myself ever having a reason to go back there. England wasn't my country. France wasn't my country. I have spoken their languages all my life, but they weren't ever truly my countries. In any case, long-distance travel is now impossible for me.

Even today, as an American citizen, I don't absolutely feel as though I have a country. My husband, Robert, makes me vote. Being able to vote sometimes does make me feel I belong. Still, I always feel strange when I check "U.S. citizen" on the census form. A woman called on the phone recently and asked if I was a U.S. citizen, and I said after a pause, "Yeah, I can say that I am." I'm sure she thought that was an odd reply. I never will feel one hundred percent American. I think you have to be born in a country, grow up in a country, to feel like a citizen. You have to be able to sing "The Star-Spangled Banner" without being able to recall exactly when you learned the words. It's not Americans who make me uncomfortable. It's my own sense of not having grown up here.

Still, along with my father, I can now say that exile was one of the best things that ever happened to me. Exile gave me a chance to live in many parts of the world, to have a chance at an education, to do whatever I wanted to do, to have freedom. Tony was right. We never would have had any such freedoms if we had stayed in Egypt.

As for the impact of displacement on my children, my daughter has said many times that she never wants to move away from Dallas. She has had enough of moving every few years. But my son is always ready to move with twenty-four hours' notice. And both of my older grandsons moved to Austin right after they graduated from high school.

I wouldn't say that this illness has heightened my sense of displacement, though it is slowly depriving me of my hard-won identity. I've quit going to church after forty years, but I'm deeply spiritual. I have a conversation with God before I go to bed every night. I think about dying, and I wonder why this illness has been inflicted on me, and I think about what happens when a person dies. I don't believe in heaven or hell, but I do believe in some kind of afterlife. Often, though, I simply pray not to die.

My mother believed in God. My father did not. My daughter believes; my brother does not. My son says he believes. I believe in a God, not necessarily a Christian God. I don't know if you return to earth again, as in reincarnation, but I believe there is an afterlife. Lately, I keep remembering my mother saying that Tony, who had already died, would come to visit her every night at the nursing home, and I keep remembering how happy that made her.

I used to fear the unknown. I was deeply disturbed when my doctor said death from this type of brain cancer, glioblastoma multiforme, is a certainty. As he repeated this fact, I got used to it. I'm not scared of dying. When I get to the point where chemotherapy doesn't work and no more surgeries are possible, I will have to come to terms with that. Right now, I pretty much don't think about it. When I quit smoking, I kept thinking about my whole life without a cigarette and I thought I couldn't do it. I had to think about taking one day at a time, and it got easier. It's that way now. I think about one day at a time. Still, I know I will die soon.

For now, I want to do something practical for other people. I wish I could deliver food to people who can't get out, but I can't drive. I keep thinking of things I could do to help others, but I'm unable to do any of them. I can't read or write anymore, but I would love to volunteer to do something useful.

I always believed that when I died I would be buried in England. But my mother is buried in a Jewish cemetery, and my father was cremated. His ashes are in a secular cemetery. For the first time in so many years, my parents couldn't find a way to be together. Since I can't be with them both, it wouldn't make sense for me to be buried over there. Anyway, I feel now that here is where I should be buried. I love my house. I would like to be buried in the back yard. At home. … Finally, home. … Home at last.

23

Finality, by Robert

2013

*M*ichele was not buried in our back yard. She selected a shady plot in an Austin cemetery not far from a house she had purchased when she returned to Austin from Washington. She was very proud of her tiny house, which was so suitable for such a petite woman. It provided a sense of security for her. She kept the house for several years after we were married so that she would not have to move into the YWCA if things did not work out with us.

Things did work out very well with us, and she picked out a house five times as large as her old house. It is located on one of the highest spots in Austin, and when she saw the 40-mile views, she said, "Buy it, Robert." When I protested that we did not even know the asking price, she replied, "Work out any details you need to. Just buy it." She sometimes had a rather simplistic problem-solving technique.

There was no way to solve her cancer problem. GBM (Glioblastoma Multiforme) is the most aggressive and deadliest form of malignant brain tumor. Three-fourths of people like Michele die in the first year. Only one percent live for three years. Practically all die within five years.

Survival for Michele was measured in days. Michele had her first seizure in February 2009. Without treatment, her life expectancy was thirty-three days. Her first major surgery was in March 2009. After she survived her first brain surgery (craniotomy), her life expectancy jumped to 179 days. After that surgery, she received radiation and chemotherapy. She was subjected to four more major surgeries and months of chemotherapy until she died on 16 February 2011. She beat the odds by living for two years with GBM.

Michele's journey for the last two years of her life is told in her blog: http://michelleprogress.blogspot.com/. Some may find it useful.

For Michele, it was a two year progression of losing the ability to write, then read, then listen to audio books, then difficulty in speaking, then not being able to speak a sentence, then only being able to say "NO!", then not even able to say that. And finally, not being able to eat during the last week as her body began to shut down.

It was a terrible experience to watch the love of my life slowly die. But her bravery and perseverance were inspiring. She never gave up. She never surrendered. An unrelenting superior force overwhelmed her.

Michele changed my life and now she is gone. She was the most interesting woman I ever met. Some of the best advice I received during my grieving period was: "Don't expect to get over your loss. Just try to get used to it." Even that is very difficult and caused considerable delay on my part in having this book finally published.

It was only through the efforts of Michele's friends, who did the transcribing, editing and proofreading, that this book has come to fruition.

RKS

-30-

End Notes

1. Booth, Martin. *Opium: A History*, 1999: St. Martin's Griffin, New York, N.Y.

2. Said, Edward. *Out of Place*. 1999: Random House, New York, NY.

3. Said. *Out of Place*.

4. Aciman, Adre. *Letters of Transit: Reflections on Exile, Identity, Language and Loss*. 1999: New Press. New York, N.Y.

5. Aciman, Andre. "Shadow Cities," an essay in *The New York Review of Books*, December 18, 1997: New York, N.Y.

6. Said, Edward. *Reflections on Exile and Other Essays*. 2001: Harvard University Press, Cambridge, Mass.

7. *Juifs d'Egypte: Images et Textes*, 1984: Editions du Scribe, Paris, France.

8. Stein, Joseph. *Fiddler on the Roof*, screenplay, 1964: New York, N.Y.

About the Authors

Photo Courtesy of: *Austin American-Statesman*

Michele Kay was born in Cairo Egypt in 1944 of a British father and a French mother. Her family was expelled from Egypt during the 1956 Suez Canal and eventually made Hong Kong and London their new residences. Michele was fluent in French and English.

She moved to the United States permanently in 1981 and became a naturalized U.S. citizen in 1997. She earned a Bachelor in Liberal Studies in 2002 and a Master's of Arts in 2005 from St. Edward's University, in Austin, Texas.

Michele was a journalist for four decades, covering politics and business for newspapers and magazines in Asia, Europe and the United States. She served as a reporter, an editor, a columnist and an editorial writer. She retired from the *Austin American-Statesman* in July 2003, and then spent three years teaching journalism at St. Edward's University. She died of an aggressive brain tumor in February 2011.

Mary Ann Roser is a native of Cincinnati, Ohio, and has been a resident of Austin since 1993. She has been a journalist for 30 years and joined the *Austin American-Statesman* in December 1995, when she met Michele Kay. Before that, she worked for the Fort Worth Star-Telegram's Austin bureau, the Knight-Ridder Washington bureau and various newspapers in Kentucky, including the *Lexington Herald-Leader* and *Owensboro Messenger-Inquirer*.

Roser has won many state and national awards, including two Knight Science Fellowships to MIT, a three-month-long fellowship to the U.S. Centers for Disease Control and Prevention and a fellowship to the National Library of Medicine.

She lives in Austin, Texas with her husband Ted.

CPSIA information can be obtained at www.ICGtesting.com
Printed in the USA
LVOW12s2350231013

358361LV00002B/189/P